NORMAN PITTENGER

Time for Consent

SCM PRESS LTD
LONDON

334 01661 4

Second, revised and enlarged edition 1970

© SCM Press Ltd 1970

Printed in Great Britain by
Richard Clay (The Chaucer Press), Ltd
Bungay, Suffolk

This book is dedicated to two friends,
whose love for one another
has shown the author the beauty and loyalty
possible in homosexual life

CONTENTS

PREFATORY NOTE

It may be useful to give a little history of the book which is here presented to the public as an SCM Press paperback.

In October 1967, there appeared from SCM Press a 'Broadsheet' entitled *Time for Consent? A Christian's Approach to Homosexuality*. That tightly-printed sixty-four page booklet forms the basis of this present book. Although the appearance of the booklet was greeted, so far as most church papers were concerned, with what has been called 'a conspiracy of silence', the printing was exhausted in about a year and a half. It was then suggested to me that it might be desirable to expand the booklet adding material about female homosexuality – since the original pamphlet concerned itself entirely with men – as well as a discussion of the legal position, information about organizations of homosexuals in this country and abroad, and even a chapter on what might be styled 'an ethic for homosexuals'. The result is now in the reader's hands: an entirely re-written, much revised, and greatly enlarged treatment of *a* Christian's approach to homosexuality. I italicize the article 'a', because I did not claim in the original 'Broadsheet', nor do I now claim, that I am speaking for the whole Christian community or dictating to the churches what their attitude ought to be. What I *am* doing is stating frankly my own view, arguing for a sympathetic attitude towards homosexuals, and attempting to state what I hope may be found a reasonable, charitable, and Christian position on the whole subject.

The 'Broadsheet' *Time for Consent?* grew out of a brief article with the same title which appeared in *New Christian* for 9 March 1967. This article was one of a series in that journal, all of them discussing various ethical issues of the present time. In the editorial preface to my article, these words were used by *New Christian*: that the following essay was a statement of the writer's belief that 'the time has come for the church to alter its attitude to homosexuals'. My article sought to make just that plea in the space of three columns of medium-sized type.

As might have been expected, I received within the next fortnight a considerable number of letters. Almost all of them were from clergymen, almost all of them were friendly to the article. Some were more than friendly: one correspondent described the article as 'a breath of fresh air' – he was an assistant curate whose work was with young men in a Midland city. A few of the letters were critical; a very few almost vituperative.

Many of those who wrote seemed to think that a development of the points in the original discussion would be valuable; it would give readers an opportunity to think through for themselves, on the basis of a more extended treatment, what I had tried to say. The result was that I expanded the five main divisions of my original draft – which for reasons of space had been somewhat curtailed when printed – and tried to present my case as clearly, although not of course as fully, as I knew how. SCM Press published this material as the 'Broadsheet' to which I have referred and which is the basis of the present book.

The publication of *Time for Consent?* brought me an enormous number of letters, while a wireless broadcast, in which I participated with several others, and an article written for *The Times* Saturday religious column, increased this flow of comments. Now I began to realize how bitter is the opposition to any attempt to write or speak sympathetically about homosexuals. For I received dozens of letters which were more than vituperative; they were hateful in attitude, consigning all homosexuals to hell and myself to utter condemnation for daring to write and publish anything kindly about 'filthy creatures', 'disgusting perverts', 'damnable sinners', and the like. Most of the letters which were of this type were from laypeople who usually began by saying such things as, 'I am a devoted churchman', 'I accept the Christian faith', or 'I am a loyal defender of the teaching of the Christian Church'. I must confess that I was shocked to discover how these correspondents, claiming to be Christians, showed none of the spirit of charity which a follower of the Lord Jesus Christ might be expected to show. I was also shocked to see how many of them had failed utterly to understand the Christian gospel; for they wrote that only when men or women confess themselves as sinners – as, in their judgement, all homosexuals must be – could they receive the grace of God. It had not occurred to them that it is always God's grace which comes *first*, his love which is *prevenient* (as theologians say) to our response, his forgiveness which awakens our repentance. Even if one agreed with them, as I do not, that homosexuality is a terrible sin, certainly the order of things in Christian faith (if the gospels and the epistles are to be trusted) is exactly the reverse of the one they adopted.

But there were many more letters which were filled with gratitude for what I had written in the pamphlet and in *The Times* article, and had said in the wireless programme. These came from dozens of clergymen as well as hundreds of laypeople – many of the latter without any church affiliation. The writers thanked me for what I had said and told me that they themselves had been trying for years to take just the attitude which I had urged. Even more moving were the scores of letters from homosexuals, both men and women. I must say something about those letters.

Without exception, they told me that they had hoped for, but despaired of, finding any Christian author who wrote understandingly about their situation. They may have had faith in God, as one of them said, but 'from the way his representatives on earth talk, I could not believe that he had any faith in me as one of his children'. My correspondents included many who were churchgoers but had always felt ill-at-ease since they knew that if members of their congregation learned of their sexual drive they would wish to exclude them from the Christian fellowship. Others wanted desperately to be Christians, to attend church services, and to receive the Holy Communion, but thought they would be rejected by the clergy and laity. Many more wrote about their love for a particular friend with whom they lived, telling me how this sharing of life and love had delivered them from promiscuity and the use of prostitutes which they had felt to be degrading or, at the best, a poor substitute for 'the real thing I have so much wanted all my life and have now found in the lover with whom I have lived' – in that particular case, for thirteen years of faithfulness.

One result of all this is that I have had the privilege of meeting and, in some instances, coming to know well a considerable number of men and women homosexuals, as had not been the case before. I found that almost without exception I *liked* them; mostly they were ordinary people, some indeed not ordinary but brilliant and gifted and highly sensitive, whose only difference from my other friends was in their sexual drive towards one of their own sex. I am more grateful than I can say for this opportunity to enlarge the circle of my acquaintance and thus to come to know so many splendid men and women whom otherwise I should never have met.

This revised and enlarged book, then, is prepared with such experiences very much in mind. I am well aware of the dangers one runs if one takes the position I do in respect to homosexuality – my experience has made that quite clear. But I am prepared to run the risk, if what I said earlier and here say at greater length can help the people for whom I feel such a deep, and I believe Christian, concern.

One last word must be said. Some who have read *Time for Consent?* have said that sections of it were 'pornographic'; and when pressed to indicate just *what* sections stressed the parts which described the nature of homosexual acts between males. To this I can only reply that if the Archbishop of Canterbury could describe these in a speech in the House of Lords during the debate on the Sexual Offences Act of 1967, I believe that a much humbler writer, whose interest is in helping others understand homosexuals, may do so. What is more, I have discovered that a very large number of people who talk about homosexuality are extremely vague about such matters; from the way in which they talk, one might conclude that what Rose Macaulay once styled in a quite different connection 'nameless orgies' are habitual among such persons. Of course any thoughtful person, one might say any human being whatsoever, should know perfectly well what 'homosexuals do' – the range of actions is fairly clear, fairly obvious, one would have thought. But evidently this is not the case. Hence I have retained in this revised book that descriptive material; and I have added a paragraph or two respecting female homosexual acts. I am unrepentant here; and I think rightly so.

In any event, here is the new book. I hope it may be of help to homosexuals in showing that Christians regard them as brothers and sisters; I hope that it may be helpful, too, for the clergy and others who share the Christian faith, suggesting to them attitudes to, and ways of assisting, homosexuals. For I am convinced that this is an important issue in our day and one which we dare not evade.

Norman Pittenger

1

INTRODUCTION

Come with me, in imagination, to a large city and spend an evening with two men whom I know well. One is in his early thirties, the other in his late twenties. They are both professional men, both successful in their work, both cultured and charming. Neither of them is in any way effeminate in manner. Yet for eight years they have lived together for one very simple reason: about ten years ago they met and fell in love. As soon as they could manage it, they set up house together. They are still as much in love now as they were then. They share their interests and they share a bed together. Since they know me well and realize that I am not likely to be shocked by what they have to tell me, they have spoken often of their love one for another and have said frankly that they 'make love' – engage in physical sexual acts – very frequently. This for them is a way in which they express their love and discover that their love is deepened by physical sharing. Both of these men are devout Christians, church-goers, and regular communicants at the Eucharist.

Now come with me to another large industrial city. Here are two men who also met by chance – both of them had been promiscuous homosexuals, seeking some release from loneliness and some way of finding physical relief by picking up partners for a 'one-night stand'. But they met each other, as it happens in a 'gay bar' in that city. They, too, fell in love. For thirteen years they have lived together, happy in their relationship with its many different aspects – but again including physical acts of love. This pair are artisans, members of a trades union, liked by their mates and accepted by them.

Both have been delivered from promiscuity, as one of them put it, by discovering a love which 'made all the difference'. They would *like* to be churchmen.

Or come to north London. Here are two women, one in her forties, the other in her late thirties. They have lived together for several years and they care deeply for each other. They wrote me asking for help: they wished to have their relationship blessed by the church of which they are devout members. What could I do to help them? they asked me.

Again, in one of the southern counties of England, visit two women in their fifties. They, too, happened to meet, both of them as teachers in a secondary school. One of them was unmarried; the other was recovering from the shock of a divorce which followed unspeakable cruelty by a demanding and irritable husband. As they talked together one day, they realized that they had met, each in the other, 'someone who understood'. They decided, after a while, to live together. After they had done this, their care for each other led almost inevitably to physical expression of their affection. As this went on, a deep love developed between them. One of them told me that when she was 'in my friend's arms', life 'became all right' and an 'unheard-of happiness' was given her. They are both churchwomen, active in the local parish, one of them teaching in a 'Sunday School' for the children. They wanted to know from me if their relationship was sinful and if their physical expression of love disqualified them from receiving the sacrament weekly, as they had been doing together.

Finally, come with me to a well-known homosexual bar in London. Watch the men there. Some of them have come to pick up a partner for a few hours of sexual activity, maybe even for a few minutes. But notice one couple who evidently have known each other for some time. See the sheer love which shines from their eyes as they talk together. Do they live in the same flat? Probably not. What do they 'do' with each other if, as one may be fairly certain, they engage in sexual activity, one with the other? You see that they have eyes for nobody but each other; you see that they are happy to be together. Is their relationship entirely wrong; is it nothing but a matter of grievous sin? How shall we regard them? Or look over there at two boys, in this case probably in their late teens. They have just met. They are obviously interested in each other. They talk for a while; then they leave the bar together. Plainly enough, they are going to the bed-sitter of one of them where they will engage in sexual activity of some sort. Are *they* wicked? Are we to reject them as 'evil-doers' who deserve *only* condemnation? What is to be our attitude towards them?

Each of these little vignettes could be repeated thousands of times in Britain, in the United States, in Canada, everywhere in the world. They present to us what is called often 'the problem of homosexuality'. How are we to approach it? What is it that makes these men and women 'tick'? Are they vastly different from the rest of the human race and to be denied elemental human rights? Are they sinners, even if (in Britain anyway) they are no longer criminals – save perhaps for the last couple, the teen-agers? It is with this question of homosexuality that this book is concerned.

Readers of a detective novel often violate the 'rules of the game'; before they have got very far into the first chapter or two of the novel, they turn to the last pages to see who committed the murder. While this spoils the story, from one point of view, they find it reassuring to have the answer before the question has been completely stated. In this discussion of homosexuality, I shall spare the reader the trouble of turning to the final pages to find out what attitude is taken towards the question of the homosexual and his place in society. I shall state here, at the very beginning, the conclusion of the argument. I can do this the more easily since in the pamphlet *Time for Consent?* of which this book is a revision and enlargement, I clearly stated my position, and I see no reason to alter my view.

I am convinced that society must accept the homosexual,

B

whether male or female, as a human being who should be accorded the same rights and privileges as are granted, without hesitation, to the heterosexual of either sex. The homosexual is different in his sexual orientation from the heterosexual; in every other respect he or she is simply another human being. He or she is not an 'abnormal' person, with 'unnatural' desires and habits; to the homosexual, the desires and habits found in that state are entirely 'normal' and 'natural' – and we have no way whatsoever of discovering any eternal standards of normality or naturalness from which such persons depart. The expression of homosexual love in physical acts of various kinds is equally 'normal' and 'natural' for a homosexual who feels such love. So much for the general *human* attitude.

As to the attitude of the Christian, and the Christian church, I am convinced that the homosexual, whether male or female, should be accepted for what he or she is. A homosexual should not be required to stop being one – that is so near to an impossibility that it is hardly worth talking about, although we shall have to say something on the subject. Neither should a homosexual be required to avoid any and every expression of love in physical ways. To ask for that is to ask the homosexual to commit sexual suicide, for unless such a man or women feels called to a celibate life (as a monk or a nun or for some other conscientious reason), it is 'natural' and 'normal' for him to wish to show love, to act in love, to 'make love', as it is equally 'natural' and 'normal' for a heterosexual to wish to do these things. The law no longer makes a homosexual male a criminal, in England at any rate, and provided he engages in physical acts with a consenting person who like himself is twenty-one or over. No problem has ever arisen in respect to homosexual women, for the older repressive laws evidently did not take them into account. But I wish to go on to say that homosexual males, as well as homosexual females, are not *sinners* either: nor should people, nor the official church, regard them as such. They are God's children, ordinary men and women, who have a particular sexual attraction different from the majority of their fellow human beings – that is all.

Bryan Magee in his interesting and helpful book *One in Twenty* (now a paperback published by Corgi Books) takes his title from his conclusion that in Britain 'one in twenty' of the population is an active homosexual. In a later chapter we shall discuss the statistical question; for the present it is sufficient to say that if Mr Magee's estimate comes anywhere near the truth the homosexual group in this land – and elsewhere in the world – is far too large to be dismissed out of hand. The fact of homosexuality, the fact of homosexuals, the fact of 'active' homosexuals (which means those who 'act' on their desires): these must be accepted for what they are. Homosexuals cannot be wished away; they cannot be dismissed as unimportant; they cannot be regarded as 'freaks', even if words like 'queers' are often applied to them. My contention is that humanly *and* Christianly we must accept them as they are and for what they are, treat them as the human beings they are, welcome them in the religious groups to which they may be attracted, and not make their lot difficult and their existence miserable by contempt, by pity, or by rejection.

When my pamphlet, mentioned above, was published, some Christian people – both lay and clerical – regarded it as bordering on pornography, while they felt that its conclusions (which I have just summed up) were a reversal of all Christian standards. We shall discuss at some length the latter criticism; that must be a central part of our argument and considerable space will be given to it. As to the former – the charge of pornography – something must be said here. The attack was made because I dared to describe, in precise terms, what homosexual males 'do' when they make love. To my mind, the attack is both absurd and short-sighted. It is absurd because it fails to recognize that very many people simply do *not* know what homosexuals 'do'; to say bluntly what are the facts is not pornographic but rather is realistic and useful. It is short-sighted because it fails to see that until we know such facts we are in no position to make *any* judgement, positive or negative, about their legitimacy. Probably the basic reason for the criticism was the fear of sexuality which still prevails in many religious circles, however enlightened these may be in other respects.

This brings me to some final remarks about the present book.

In my earlier pamphlet I confined myself to homosexual men and their problems. But the enormous correspondence which I received after its publication made it clear to me that what I had to say was welcome to and important for women who are lesbians – female homosexuals. I have been invited to speak to their organizations; I have come to know, as I did not know before, a considerable number of lesbians; and I am frank to say that to them I should wish to apply what I had said about the male homosexuals whom I knew – generally speaking, they are a decent, brave, honest group, with an urgent desire for acceptance and understanding from their fellow-citizens. There are some 'promiscuous' lesbians just as there are some, maybe a considerable number, of 'promiscuous' homosexual men. There are some who will resort to prostitutes for sexual satisfaction, just as there are some, and maybe many more, men who will do so. But by and large, I am now certain – on the basis not of theory, speculation or prejudice, but of actual acquaintance, frank conversation, and close observation – that they, like their brothers, are for the most part fine, upright, moral (if not *conventionally* 'moral') people. I am including them in my discussion in this book because I want to help them – and because I want the Christian community to help them, too.

Then I wish to emphasize that in this book I am taking for granted the goodness of human sexuality. Something will be said about this in the appropriate place. But here and now I wish to say clearly and precisely that sexuality is a good thing, a God-given thing, a wonderful and beautiful thing. Of course it can be perverted, as can everything else in human experience; but I see no reason whatsoever for thinking that the conscientious and self-accepting homosexual, or any homosexual of any sort, is by the mere fact of his or her homosexuality perverting sexuality. We shall be seeing what the perversion or distortion of sexuality really means in a basically Christian context; what it does *not* mean is simply being homosexual and wishing urgently to express one's homosexuality.

But, it may be said, historically the Christian tradition has regarded homosexuality as in fact a perversion or distortion. I know that perfectly well. But it does not lead me to change my view. This is not because I have the foolhardiness or the presumption to claim that some new revelation of truth has been given to me and to the hundreds of Christian clergymen and laypeople who have written to tell me that they agree with me. The reason for my contradiction of the generally accepted position in past ages is based on something else. It is the consequence of the honest recognition that we today possess many more facts about the subject, hence are able to make a saner and more balanced judgement, than our forbears. To say this is simply to state a fact. Furthermore, my 'permissive' attitude on the subject, as some may think it to be, is derived from taking with utmost seriousness the possibility that in our own day the Holy Spirit may have led us to understand more profoundly important truths about men and women which an earlier age, through no fault of its own, could not understand. It is not at all difficult to see how the traditional attitude developed, out of what earlier ideas, in what circumstances, and in the light of what views of human nature were then naturally accepted – indeed taken for granted. But we may feel obliged to disagree; many of us do.

That first couple, those two pairs of women in Britain, that man and his friend in the Midlands, the lovers in the London bar, the two adolescents – those people with whom we began this introductory chapter - what are we to do about them – say to them?

In the past, the women would have been disregarded, but the men would have been thought of as 'dirty perverts', to use the phrase of an ecclesiastical dignitary who has written to me. The boys would be brought to book and told that they must each of them hunt for a girl if they wanted to have sexual experience – that would be 'natural' and 'normal', an adviser would have said, while physical acts with males were only evil. Certainly none of them, had the truth been known, would have been welcomed 'to church' or permitted to play an active part in the affairs of the parish or congregation to which perchance they belonged.

More recently, they would have been taken as pathetically 'sick people', who should be 'cured' of their malady, whether by psychological methods or in some other way. They would have been regarded with pity for being what they are; if not rejected, they would have been 'helped' to stop being themselves.

This book is a protest against *both* these views. As the reader will see, I cannot accept the notion that homosexuals are 'sick' people, simply because they are what they are – although, like everybody else, they may be 'sick' in other ways or because of anxieties and troubles which society has created for them. And certainly they are not 'dirty perverts', whatever an ecclesiastic may say. The very use of such words to describe a fellow human-being makes anything else such a person says irrelevant and meaningless. What is more, terms like that accord ill with the spirit of him who showed unfailing compassion and care for others – that One whom even this ecclesiastical dignitary certainly regards as his Lord and Master.

Somewhere Albert Camus, the French novelist tragically killed a few years ago in a motor-car accident, wrote these words: 'I am against those who think they are absolutely right'. The conviction of what someone has styled 'my own remarkable rightness' is bound to lead to the kind of judgemental attitudes that make real understanding and profound sympathy impossible. We have been told – I think correctly

– that religious faith *must* include an element of doubt. Otherwise it is not faith at all, but the pretence to *knowledge*. Yet as St Paul told us, we 'walk by faith', not by the kind of absolute certainty which knowledge might be thought to provide. So also with moral judgements.

The man or woman who is so convinced of his own moral rectitude that he cannot *see* other human beings as human beings, but only their defection from his own 'standards', whatever they may be, is in my view a sorry specimen of the human race and (should this position be linked with Christian religious faith) a poor specimen of the Christian fellowship. But I must be careful lest I myself fall into the judgemental attitude; and my only way of avoiding that mistake is to recognize that even those who disagree with me – those who, to take a very concrete example, have written to me calling me 'a dirty man', 'a person who incites young men to sin', 'a false prophet', or 'a filthy defender of pornography' – are, like myself, 'conditioned' by their background and upbringing. This is not to deny human freedom; it is only that the limits of our freedom are imposed by our circumstances. Yet I find it difficult to understand how people who have written to me in this manner, usually without reading *Time for Consent?* in its pamphlet form but depending on certain journalistic reports of what it was supposed to contain, can so insistently claim that *they* and *they only* have what one of them dared to call (in Pauline phrase) 'the mind of Christ'. Such 'absolute rightness' seems to me incredible. What is much more serious, especially when applied to the problem with which this book is concerned, it seems to me a terrible and frightening denial of Christ's compassion and the loving awareness which must mark those who claim to be his disciples.

I write at such length on this matter because the condemnatory view taken by these people has made it impossible for them to have *any* real awareness of what makes a homosexual, be it a girl or a boy, a man or women, the sort of person each of them is. If we condemn another man out-of-hand we shall never be able to know what makes him 'tick'. Furthermore, it is apparent that a very considerable number, probably the majority, of those who are free with their condemnation have never really known intimately an active homosexual. They are content to repeat the words which describe some imagined stereotype: words like 'pansy', 'fairy', 'pervert', etc., with their correlative terms like 'sexually obsessed', 'seducer of the young', 'filthy violator of others' – these are the terms that I find in the criticisms of my plea for charitable understanding. Their picture of the homosexual is drawn from various sources, but it is the picture of a man who looks and acts like a woman, or who cannot keep his hands from indecent fondling of any other male, or who spends his evenings in resorts where he finds willing sexual partners, or who frequents public conveniences to 'pick up' a companion; or it is of a women who pretends to be a man, or seduces every girl she can discover, or who offends public taste in some other way. Usually, it is a man who is in view; and here the stereotype is the most lurid.

Now it so happens that I know many homosexuals of both sexes. My acquaintance was fairly minimal when I first wrote about their problem; since then, thanks to the numbers who have turned to me for such assistance as they thought I might be able to give them – just because I had written sympathetically and they were overjoyed to find such sympathy – I have come to know reasonably well a very large number of men and women who in this respect deviate from the accepted social norm in sexual desires and practices. And I can say with assurance that the stereotype is *false*.

Of course there are the promiscuous types, especially among men. Of course some homosexuals are unpleasant people. Of course there are those who *faute de mieux* resort to the employment of prostitutes. But these are by no means the typical homosexual. We shall say more about this in later chapters; but here and now I must insist that the 'run-of-the-mill' homosexual male, as well as the ordinary homosexual woman, is a very different sort of person from that stereotype. Most of those whom I have come to know are entirely decent people, coming from all classes of society, working in all sorts of trades or professions, not at all 'obvious' or 'blatant'. Indeed, it is almost impossible to identify who is or who is not a homosexual, simply by looking at him or her.

I have gone with a friend to a very well-known homosexual bar in London, to try to determine what if anything is common to all male homosexuals. Had it not been that practically everybody in that bar was a man – there were three or four women, with companions, who may or may not have been lesbians or who may simply have dropped in without awareness of the sort of establishment this was – there was *nothing* to distinguish most of the patrons. A very few, among the perhaps hundred men not more than half-a-dozen, were rather effeminate in manner. Otherwise, those present were very ordinary-looking and all were entirely well-behaved. They made friends more readily, they spoke more easily to others whom they had not previously known, they had a greater *camaraderie* than is usually the case. Probably some of them would have been more cynical or sarcastic – homosexuals would say 'bitchy' – but this was not obvious to a visitor. And there are vast numbers who do not frequent such places at all; they do not enjoy 'the gay scene', as they would put it, but prefer to be quietly at home or with their friends.

Further, the number of men and women who have been able to establish fairly permanent relations with another of their own sex is much larger than is generally known. These relationships may not last for the whole of the life-time of the partners, although often enough they do; they may be for a few months or a few years, during which the couple either try to live together or spend their free hours together. Some sort of *modus vivendi* has been worked out between them, even when one of the partners tends to become more promiscuous after a period of faithfulness to the other.

But I have yet to meet a homosexual man or women who did not *want* permanence, deep down in his inner desiring. I am now sure that like all other human beings, the homosexual wants to give and to receive genuine love – if by love we mean commitment of self, sharing of life, openness to another. With that love they wish to enjoy the physical actions which express it; but so do most heterosexuals. In other words, to sum up what I am urging, the homosexual is not very different from the majority of his brothers and sisters.

Much in this introductory chapter is only assertion. That I acknowledge. The remainder of this book will be a development and argument for these assertions, backed by such information and by such specifically Christian convictions as I am able to offer. But until we get rid of the irrational prejudices which so often characterize those who condemn or reject or laugh at the homosexuals, we shall fail completely to understand – and failing in understanding, we shall resemble the Pharisees of the gospel narratives, whose proud self-righteousness made them unable to grasp the truth about their fellows or to enter into genuinely human relationships with them.

2

THE SITUATION TODAY

Homosexuality has become a much more obvious fact in recent years than it has been in the past. In the large cities, but also in smaller communities, the presence of homosexuals, especially males, is an inescapable matter of observation. One way of indicating this is the appearance of 'cartoons' in the popular journals in which jokes appear that apply to homosexuals and their relationships – something that in an older day would have been quite impossible. For anybody with his eyes open, it is apparent that the way in which many people talk together is often an equally clear indication. Within the last few years there have been a number of plays and films which deal with the theme; and they deal with it not as something extraordinary or unfamiliar but as well-known to the audience in the theatre. The publishers' lists each year include novels that openly and frankly portray homosexuals – indeed it might be said that this sort of writing has become almost a fashionable thing.

There is no reason to think that there are actually many more homosexuals, male or female, than there have been in the past, although some observers have thought that there is some increase in numbers. However this may be, their presence among us has been brought to the attention of the general public in a fashion quite unparalleled, at least in the recent history of the western world. Furthermore, there is an increasing recognition that no longer can the homosexual condition and tendency be dismissed. These are men and women whose personal integrity and honesty demand, as more and more people agree, that they be considered in as sympathetic a way as we can manage and with as much understanding of their condition as is possible for those whose sexual inclinations are heterosexual.

In England the liberalizing of the law in respect to homosexual acts in private between consenting males of twenty-one and over has been accomplished. Based largely on the findings of the Wolfenden commission, this means (as we shall point out in some detail in a later chapter) that such acts are no longer criminal. Certain special provisions are made for men in the armed forces and the merchant navy; what are often styled 'safeguards' are set up for persons under twenty-one. But in general the same freedom which is granted the heterosexual to behave sexually as he wishes is accorded the homosexual, at least so far as the law is concerned. In other English-speaking countries the legal situation is different, although even there (notably in Canada, for example) efforts are being made to effect a similar liberalization. For women who are homosexually inclined, there seems never to have been any legal prohibition; hence there has been and is no need to have legislation which permits the same freedom for them.

In the movement for this change in respect to the law, strong support was given by representatives of most religious bodies in England, not least from the Church of England. This support came as a great surprise to many people, since to them it seemed quite extraordinary that ecclesiastical dignitaries, distinguished theologians, and professional exponents of Christian moral theology, should interest themselves in what to these people seemed a remarkable relaxation of moral standards and an altogether too permissive attitude towards what they regarded as serious deviation from the conventional Christian ethical position. But of course the reason for the support from such religious leaders was that they knew very well the grave injustice of the older legal restriction, while they had also become convinced that in matters of sexual behaviour the Christian position, whatever that might be, must be ready to stand on its own feet and commend itself by its own intrinsic merit. It must no longer rely on what in the Middle Ages would have been called 'the secular arm' to enforce this standard on every citizen, regardless of his religious allegiance or his complete lack of religious commitment.

In none of the speeches or articles which I have read, in nothing spoken or written by the distinguished churchmen to whom I have just referred, could be found any commendation of homosexuality. On the contrary, they seem to have gone out of their way, very likely from strategic purposes as well as from personal conviction, to make clear that they abhor homosexuality. But they did not think, or at least this is what their utterances seem to indicate, that physical expressions of homosexuality should properly be described as *criminal* acts. They regarded such acts as having the nature of *sin*, to be sure; but they did not think that sin was a matter for legal enactment.

One of the objects of the article in *New Christian*, upon which my present discussion is based, was to suggest and urge another point of view on the matter. The question is: granted that homosexual acts are not criminal, are they *sinful*? It has been generally accepted in religious circles that they are. My belief is that in and of themselves they are *not*. I have just written, 'in and of themselves', a phrase which is intended to qualify the apparently blanket statement that homosexual physical contacts are *never* sinful. My purpose was to say, 'it all depends . . .' And I shall try, in the sequel, to make clear what that means; in other words, I shall seek to consider such acts in their context, with respect to the intention with which they are undertaken and in the light of what seems to me the only possible understanding for us today of the nature of man and of the meaning of human sin.

This will require that we discuss the Christian view of human nature and of the 'will of God' for men. It will also require that we give attention to the concept of sin as this has been understood by most Christians for a large part of Christian history, and contrast it with a more modern attitude as to what constitutes sinfulness – an attitude which, although it is indeed 'more modern', may also claim with justice to be more in accordance with what Jesus himself said and did. Only in the context of such a wider reference is it possible to come to grips with the question posed above: if homosexual acts are not criminal, are they sinful?

But before we undertake that task, we must see more of the contemporary situation. We must come to terms with the fact that a very considerable number of men and women *are* latently or overtly homosexual rather than heterosexual. The number is not *very* large in comparison with the vast majority of men and women who are heterosexual, but in actual statistical terms it is sufficient to warrant careful attention.

These statistics are not often easy to come by. Even when we have them, they are hard to interpret. Various studies in this country and in the United States have attempted to work out reliable figures; and from such surveys it would appear that a fairly safe estimate would be that perhaps five per cent of the total population in the United Kingdom, in the United States, and in Canada may be classified as homosexual in some sense. This would suggest that in Britain there are between two and two-and-a-half million men and women whose sexual drive is towards persons of their own sex. In the United States, there would be rather more than nine million and in Canada something under one million.

It should be understood that these surveys, made by sociologists and other experts, include both latent homosexuals and active homosexuals. By *latent* here I mean men and women who for the most part do not engage in any physical acts of a homosexual sort, although they may have done so at one time or, at long intervals, they may still seek such a contact. By *active* I mean men and women who with a fair degree of frequency have sexual relations with a member of their own sex. It would be my guess – and nothing more than a guess – that there are something like a million-and-a-half men and women in the United Kingdom who belong to the latter group, while in the United States there might be some six million and in Canada seven hundred thousand. This guess is based on no reliable evidence and represents only my personal impression of the number of active homosexuals in relation to the total number of persons who may be classified in a more general sense as belonging to the homosexual population.

If anything like this number of men and women are homosexuals who with a fair degree of frequency seek and find an outlet for their sexual drive by physical contacts with other persons of their own sex, we have to reckon with a not insignificant proportion of the total populations of the countries which I have mentioned. In other lands the figures are probably similar and in some countries, notably perhaps in the Latin world and in Scandinavia, the figures may be rather higher.

One clear indication of the large number of homosexuals is the existence or more and more periodicals especially edited and written for the homosexual reader. Such publications contain stories, essays, poems, news sections, all of a type that will have a homosexual appeal. Sometimes the material contained in them is shoddy and cheap; sometimes it reaches the level of quite respectable literature. More will be said about these periodicals in a later chapter. For the moment, it may be pointed out that certain of the publications print photographs, drawings, or other artistic representations with the same particular appeal; these may include pictures of men and women scantily dressed or totally nude, often with the genital organs plainly visible. Legal restrictions prevent a very wide circulation of such publications, yet they are available for those who will take the trouble and run the risk. In addition, periodicals printed and published in certain continental countries, especially Denmark and Sweden, are obtainable, although with greater difficulty, outside those lands; these tend to be much bolder, both in their written material and in their photographic and art representations. It is probable that no very large proportion of the homosexual population is interested in any of these; I mention them to show that there *is* a public for them and that this public is quite explicitly a homosexual public. Publishers presumably find them profitable to produce.

Still another manifestation of homosexuality is the appearance, in certain publications in this country and in North America, of advertisements from men or women, seeking through such a medium to find friends who share their interests. Sometimes these journals are not explicitly homosexual in appeal; that they include such advertisements, along with others for heterosexual contacts, is a sign that more and more homosexual persons are prepared to do something about their condition. It is also important to notice the increasing number of novels in which the homosexual theme is handled with great frankness and openness. Unquestionably the general reading public welcomes such books because they have literary merit – the novels of James Baldwin, especially *Giovanni's Room* and *Another Country*, illustrate this in North America, while such works as Mary Renault's *The Charioteer* do the same in Britain. These are mentioned only as examples; but what they show is that many readers are interested in a portrayal of the homosexual and his or her problems. There is no question of the special appeal of such novels for the person who knows homosexuality from the inside, so to say, and who finds pleasure in books that tell of people with the same drive. Once again, then, we have a pointer to the presence in our midst of a considerable number of persons who must be classified as homosexual.

It is also evident that the homosexual is much more obviously part of the social scene today. Certain sections of large cities make this plain enough. The homosexual is not easily identifiable in most cases; but those who are 'in the know' can readily recognize them. Where there are large numbers of homosexuals in a given area, this is apparent. And the increase in the number of 'gay bars', especially in big towns or metropolitan centres, is also noteworthy – as is the publication, for those interested, of 'guides' to such places for visitors to these towns or cities.

However many men or women there may be who can love only a person of their own sex, their existence then is so much a part of our contemporary world that it can no longer be denied, minimized, or neglected. They are very much here; their presence must be taken very seriously. What sort of people are they?

My impression is that they are *all sorts* of people. They may be adolescents or very young men or women; they may be middle-aged or elderly. They may be lorry-drivers or they may be bank directors. They may be professional women or they may be shop-assistants. It is impossible to think of any social class, occupation, financial position, or other grouping by which sociologists categorize human beings, which does not contain its percentage of homosexuals. At one time, it was assumed that only actors, literary people, artists, or 'the idle rich' were likely to be homosexual; nowadays we know that this is not the case. Certainly these professions contribute their share of the homosexual population, but equally many other professions and ranks make their contribution too. In Mr Magee's book, to which we have already made reference, the author reported that in the various homosexual bars and clubs which he visited in obtaining the material for his broadcasts and his book, he found people of all types and of all ages. Furthermore he reported that after he had pursued his enquiries for several months he became aware of the fact that several of his journalistic colleagues, and others whom he had always thought to be completely heterosexual, belonged in the company of homosexuals. His judgement was entirely sound, I believe, for my own experience, after writing my original article, confirms Mr Magee's conclusions in every respect. A very considerable number of men and women have confided

c

in me because they felt that I understand their situation. It has been astonishing to see how varied are their backgrounds, their jobs, their educational experience, their financial condition, their age.

But with that variety, I know that to come to some sympathetic awareness one must try to see their actual common situation – the particular characteristics they share, their feelings and affections, and the sort of sexual fulfilment of human potentiality which seems to them the only way in which they can realize themselves as human beings. Across all the differences in profession and age, in education and culture, there are some *constants* with which we must concern ourselves; hence the later chapter on the homosexual condition.

One thing stands out very clearly. The homosexual is not necessarily, by his or her very nature, a promiscuous person or one who wishes to make use of male or female homosexual prostitutes. Many do; or some do. But there does not seem to be an *essential* difference here between heterosexual promiscuity and homosexual promiscuity, or between the use of prostitutes of one's own sex and the use of prostitutes of the other sex. One can understand what drives some men and some women into promiscuous relationships or into the use of prostitutes, whether of the same or of the opposite sex. This does not mean that everybody engages in such practices; nor does it mean that we must approve of them. One must always care deeply for the men and women who are involved, knowing that they are human beings worthy of our respect, if not of our admiration. Yet such caring for the persons need not imply that one approves of what they do. Nor do all homosexuals approve of their friends or other homosexuals who act in this fashion.

Another matter which strikes one is that despite the patent differences between male homosexuals and female homosexuals, there is a considerable similarity between them, too. It would be absurd to minimize the differences and expect that they are of no consequence in the total adjustment of the person to his condition. Yet the very fact that for homosexuals of both sexes, the particular *attrait* is towards a member of the same sex, rather than to a member of the other sex, does establish the similarity, if not the identity, between them. To refer once again to my own experience, discussions with groups of male homosexuals and of female homosexuals have made it plain that many, although not all, of their problems are similar – the one outstanding difference, I have discovered, is that women have a much stronger and more conscious longing for permanence in a relationship; although I must add that deep within the male homosexual, I am convinced, there is an equal yearning for permanence, even if it is not so vividly and consciously felt.

To many it may seem strange that there is that longing. When we consider how difficult it is to establish such a permanent relationship, especially in western society as it is now organized and with the prevailing attitude towards homosexuality in general, it is remarkable that there are so many attempts to achieve permanence. Despite relaxation in the law, despite the change in attitude towards homosexuals, it is not easy for two men to live together. There seems little concern about two women who do this – it is difficult to understand the reason for the difference in attitude in this respect, save that most people appear to think that women are not likely to be thus deeply in love with other women nor wish to engage in sexual relations with them. Similarly, nobody is offended when two women dance together, while it is thought to be outrageous if two men do so.

Although it is not easy for two men to share rooms and to be known as intimately related with each other, the situation today is immeasurably better than in past years. My own first knowledge of homosexuality, apart from school talk and awareness of school experimentation with members of one's own sex, came when a highly respected and prosperous man, in the community where my family lived, was hounded to death – quite literally, since the ostracism and contempt which he suffered brought on a serious nervous exhaustion which ended in death from a heart attack – after it had become known that the slightly younger man with whom he had been living in an attractive house on the outskirts of the town was not his 'nephew', as had been given out, but his 'lover'. The couple had lived together for at least ten years in that house and before that time for many years elsewhere. They were both decent men, churchgoers, active in community affairs, generous with their money in support of charitable enterprises; in every way they were ideal citizens. Yet so soon as gossip had started and had been confirmed by a remark or two dropped by someone who claimed that he had seen them embracing on one occasion, they were ostracized, no longer invited to visit supposed friends in the community, talked about behind their backs, often treated with open contempt.

It was a terrible tragedy. As an adolescent I did not at first grasp what it was all about. I had seen both of the men, although as it happened my family were not personally acquainted with them. They came to our parish church every Sunday and had been popular with those who met and knew them. Why, then, I wondered, had they disappeared from sight? Why did older people give each other knowing looks when either of them was mentioned in conversation? Oddly enough, it was the local parson who explained the matter to me. I have forgotten what was the occasion, but I remember his remarking to a group of young men who acted as acolytes or servers, me among them, that 'Mr So-and-so had been "living in sin" with Mr So-and-so, and had been "found out"'. It did not take long for us boys to grasp what was meant; we talked about it a little, but without any profound understanding. Now, when I think back to the whole incident, I feel what an appalling waste of life, what a needless tragedy, and what a judgement on those who themselves presumed to judge, the whole episode really was.

Nowadays something like this would not be likely to

happen, perhaps. Yet the threat of it is always there; and sensitive homosexuals, aware of that threat, are likely to be afraid of openly living together, especially in a town of ten or fifteen thousand people where they may be exposed to nasty gossip. In a large city, like London or one of the great provincial cities, or New York or some other American metropolis, things are very different. A certain degree of privacy is assured; in any event, neighbours are not much interested in those living next to them or even living in the same block of flats.

The strange side of the episode I have recalled is that had the two men been non-churchgoers, had they been persons who did not share a permanent house but met only occasionally, or had they been the type of homosexual who is discreetly promiscuous, nothing would have happened. The very fact that they were faithful to each other and evidently very much in love was counted against them. Thus society managed to condemn an arrangement which was certainly better than might have been the case had they been the sort who engage only in 'one-night stands'. Perhaps this helps to point a moral about the damage which conventional morality, lacking any real understanding, can do to human beings. Perhaps it helps also to enable us to see that the newer attitude of acceptance has something to be said for it, even for those who do not like homosexuals or homosexuality and regard the whole thing as a disagreeable business.

The reference to the religious attitude of the men whom I have just mentioned leads me to say that it is noteworthy that a very large proportion of persons who without hesitation will acknowledge their homosexuality to a trusted friend or counsellor are deeply religious people. This may come as a great surprise to those who assume that the homosexual, almost by definition, is a sinful person who has no use for religion because it may interfere with his sexual activities or interests. It may also surprise those who think that religion and the conventional moral pattern are identical. Yet the plain fact is that many homosexuals are not only religious people but are or would like to be church-going people, too. I suspect that not a few of them do not expect that they would continue to be welcome in the worship and life of the religious community if their sexual feelings were known; indeed I *know* this to be the case. For this reason they hide these feelings from others in a way even more careful and prudent than would normally be the case. A great many others yearn for the opportunity to express their profound religious instinct, but have the not unjustified belief that the religious institutions would not really wish to have them participate fully in their activities, once it was realized that the kind of sexual life which they enjoyed was not the accepted sort.

I had not expected the considerable number of letters that I received from clergymen who have written to me informing me that they have known many young men, as well as older ones, who wished desperately to have some attachment to the Christian church – men who in the confessional or in private and confidential conversation acknowledged their homosexuality, sometimes saying quite frankly that they were living with and engaging in occasional or frequent physical relations with another man. So also with women. Such letters confirm my opinion that homosexuals are like most human beings in this respect also. They are not *anti-religious*. They often wish to *be* religious, even to the extent of taking their place in the life of some religious group. Their problem here is in part the same as that of the rest of the population – the conventional presentation of Christian belief seems to them so tied up with incredible notions that they find the whole enterprise intellectually and n other ways alien to their experience and to their thinking as modern men. But they *wish* it were otherwise. And for the homosexual there is the added difficulty that he is never sure of his *place* in a religious body. Will it accept him or reject him? Will he find a welcome or the 'cold shoulder'? If by any chance, through some unfortunate bit of gossip, his sexual proclivities become known to the clergymen or to a church official, will he be told (quietly, yet forcibly) that he can no longer be an active member unless he gives up all expression of his sexual instinct?

At this point I am not arguing one way or the other so far as the programme or policy of religious groups is concerned; I am only stating the case and describing the situation. At the very least, it is a tragedy for homosexuals, and for the Christian church in its several branches, that such fear should be strongly felt. Even if one granted that homosexual acts are indeed grievous sin, it would seem that the teaching which as a child I received – that the church *exists for sinners* – would demand a different attitude. But more of this at a later point.

I am very conscious of the charge which may be made – that in what has been written so far I have been guilty of romanticizing the homosexual. To this I should reply that my own wonder is about how well the critic himself knows homosexuals, whether they be men or women. One discovers that most of the people who describe the homosexual as a nasty person have little if any acquaintance with men and women with this sexual drive; in several instances I have enquired about this and learned that the most violent attacks came from those who admitted under questioning that they were not closely acquainted with anybody who was an acknowledged homosexual.

Furthermore, I am well aware of the presence among homosexuals of much that is sordid and unpleasant – and homosexuals often admit this very honestly. Yet there is not much more of such sordidness and unpleasantness among them than among heterosexuals. Once one gets over one's distaste, which many certainly feel, at the thought of men or women engaging in any sort of specifically homosexual physical relations; once one gets over the disgust, which some strongly feel, about the particular acts in which homosexuals may engage, one comes to see that homosexuals are really quite ordinary human beings. Some of them are educated and cultured, others are not; some are interesting, others are not; some are agreeable companions, others are not. In fact, they are so much like ordinary people that most of the time it is quite literally impossible to 'tell a homosexual when one sees him'. There is no special external sign; by no means are all homosexuals of the 'pansy' or 'dyke' sort, although of course a few are. Not many of them dress in an odd way, although some may do so. Few of them are obviously 'over-sexed' as the saying goes, although some of them are that way.

A recent American study of homosexuals, published in this country by the SCM Press (H. Kimball Jones, *Toward a Christian Understanding of the Homosexual*), has gone far to show that relatively few homosexuals are promiscuous. This, too, will seem to many an astonishing revelation, for they have taken it for granted that the average male homosexual, whatever may be said of women with such a sexual inclination, is *always* promiscuous, seeking any man or boy with whom he can have sexual relations – perhaps especially the latter, since there is a strange and (as we now know, from practically every expert on the subject) erroneous idea that such men delight in the seduction of boys who are adolescent or younger. As a matter of fact, the average male homosexual prefers partners of his own age or perhaps *slightly* younger or older; and he wants, sometimes quite desperately, to have a relationship which, far from being promiscuous, will be as nearly permanent as he can make it.

The aspect of homosexual life which is associated in the public mind with the frequenting of public conveniences in search of a temporary partner has been very much exaggerated. Of course there *are* men who frequent such places. But as the admirable Quaker pamphlet, *Towards a Quaker View of Sex*, remarked, it is highly probable that these persons in many instances have felt themselves driven to such expedients because society has made a different approach not only difficult but often impossible for them. In this book, however, I am not concerned with this sort of person; I am writing about the ordinary, decent, well-behaved, and (as one might say) 'conscientious' homosexual. At the same time, I should wish to plead for an understanding, sympathetic attitude on the part of religious leaders, priests, pastors, and confessors, towards the type of homosexual who does get into trouble in this way. One need not condone; one ought to try to grasp the condition of such men, their loneliness, their need, and then seek to help them.

We now turn to a consideration of human nature and its meaning, as this may be understood by the Christian believer. Then we shall move on to a discussion of human sin; and after that to a treatment of the homosexual condition, the physical acts associated with it, the various agencies and organizations which work for or with the homosexual, the legal situation in which he finds himself. Finally, we shall devote two chapters to what may be styled the morality of homosexual behaviour and a possible ethic for the self-confessed homosexual.

3

WHAT IS MAN?

There are many different ways in which people have sought to describe or define what it means to be a man. Some of these are patently unchristian. It has been held that man is nothing more than a somewhat complicated animal, whose mental capacity, such as it is, bears the sort of relationship to his animality that the smoke rising from a steam-engine bears to the operation of the engine; mind is purely and simply epiphenomenal. On the other hand, it has been held that man is essentially a 'soul' or a 'spirit', who for a short time is obliged to inhabit a physical body. This view, although it has sometimes been regarded as peculiarly 'religious', is utterly contrary to a genuinely Christian position. It is altogether *too* spiritual and might better be styled a variety of the 'gnosticism' of the first centuries of our era – a way of regarding the world which, for what it took to be the greater glory of God, looked at the body and all that is material or physical in the world of experience with disdain and dislike.

Dismissing both these descriptions as impossible of acceptance by anyone who in the slightest degree grasps the basic biblical view of God and the world, we come to the position classically enunciated by Boethius and adopted by St Thomas Aquinas.

'Man is an individual substance of a rational nature.' In this case, it is the human capacity to reason, to be rational, which establishes man as different from the animals, although in respect to his body he belongs unquestionably among them. About this I should say that it is indeed true that man has

some capacity to think and that he can be *more or less* rational;
were this not so, we should hardly be able to engage in any
meaningful discourse or to put our confidence in any
statements claiming to be true. Yet it has been pointed out,
quite correctly, that even the animals, at a certain level,
appear to have a limited capacity for thought, although this
is not developed in the way in which with men it is known
to have been sharpened and made increasingly competent.

Some have been silly enough to argue that man is the only
self-conscious creature. But here again, we now know that
there are approximations to self-consciousness in the animal
world; and that the fact that man has both such awareness
and with it an unusual capacity for introspection will not of
itself differentiate him entirely from other creatures. Again,
many have claimed that the human species is the only one to
show moral responsibility. Yet it now appears that in the
so-called 'higher animals' there are glimmerings of a moral
sense, with its accompaniment in a feeling (however dim)
of responsibility. This, of itself, seriously damages the
contention that man is differentiated specifically by his
being a moral creature.

I do not wish to deny that there is a considerable element of
truth in all these views, provided they are stated cautiously
and with due qualification. But I should urge that what
brings them all together and gives them their distinctively
human quality is what I take to be the central truth about
man: that he is *created to be* and *is* a *lover*. By this I mean
that whatever may be the *suggestions* of a capacity to love in
other species, with some vague intimations and adumbra-
tions of the human experience of mutuality in tenderness and
the elements present in love, the way in which this quality
is dominant in all men – and that, in spite of the appearances
of the opposite, or as we might well say precisely *because of*
those appearances, which psychologists tell us are the
consequence of a fear of 'being caught out' in love – is of
such a high degree, of a degree so immense, that in practice
it amounts to a genuine difference in kind.

But it may be asked whether something of the same sort, in respect to a very high degree of difference, has not already been admitted for rationality, self-consciousness, and moral sense. The answer is 'yes'; but the point I wish to make is that none of these is the *dominant* quality in man. His dominant quality, which in Whiteheadian language might be called the 'monarchical principle' in the organization or patterning of his existence, is *love*. Of this I am convinced; and that not only on Christian grounds, but because of the extraordinary way in which psychological study, not least in Freud with his emphasis on the *libido* as the fundamental drive in every human life, has demonstrated the fact. The genuinely integrating factor in human experience is the capacity to give love and to be loved.

Hence man is to be defined or described as a *lover* – he is created to love, his deepest intentionality is that he shall love, his manhood is expressed in his loving. That is my first contention. My second, which will be developed in the next chapter, is that *as* a lover man is both frustrated and also liable to distortion and twisting – this latter is his *sin*. I have said 'liable'; it would be more accurate to say that the present existential situation of each man is precisely inclusive of such distortion and twisting. But of this more will be said shortly.

My third contention is that man, created to be a lover, but now frustrated and twisted in his loving, can be *released to love* as he is intended to love. This is what our Christian talk of redemption, atonement and reconciliation is all about. We could state this in various ways, ways as various as have been the theories of atonement in Christian history. But each of the ways is a significant symbol for something deep in human experience as this has been Christianly interpreted. Each of these symbols has been drawn from some particular pattern of ideas which was entertained by people living at a given time and place. The awareness of 'wrongness' in themselves was portrayed in such terms. For one age, evil powers entered into and perverted human life; in another, corruptibility and mortality destroyed the integrity of manhood; for still another, disobedience to what was taken to be divine law was the problem; for the Middle Ages, it was servitude or slavery. For Abelard and for many moderns (including the present writer) the root of man's difficulty is the presence of frustration in loving, coupled with the sure fact that in such loving as one can manage one is misdirected and impotent. Today, for a considerable number of men and women the analogy for this would be their awareness of mental or emotional disorder. But the significance of each of these ways of approaching the matter is that it points to the fact that release *is* given, freedom *is* granted (with whatever qualifications and conditions may surround it), and alienation *has been* overcome, through Jesus Christ.

Christian faith proclaims that all this has been accomplished, not by man's own efforts and most certainly not through 'works', but by the generously given and freely operative 'grace of God' – which is to say, by God's Love in action in his world. That Love has been embodied, enfleshed, enmanned – made a vivid historical reality – under the conditions of a full and complete human life in the total event which is called by the name of Jesus Christ. Such is the gospel. Such is the centre of Christian faith. In Christ, as in no other place and at no other time, the divine Love is operative for *man*, in man's *own* terms and in man's *own* language. He is 'the disclosure in act', as the Anglo-American philosopher A. N. Whitehead put it in his *Adventures of Ideas*, of 'what Plato divined in theory': namely, that divine 'persuasion' or Love is the deepest, highest, most real thing in the cosmos; indeed, that the cosmos is grounded in that 'persuasion' or Love. Hence the event of Jesus Christ reveals, not by some mere pictorial representation nor by the drawing aside of a veil, but by the full activity of a man who is brother to all men, 'the divine nature and the divine agency in the world', to quote again from Whitehead. All that is best in human nature responds to this, or can be brought to respond to it; and this response is by free assent and acceptance and not by coercive pressure or the compulsion of power. The 'deep' in man, which is nothing other than the image of God in him, is enabled to say 'Amen' to the deepest in the cosmos and, more than that, to God himself as 'pure, unbounded Love'. The preparation for this, and the persuasive action within human nature which brings about such conformity of the *within* to the *beyond*, is called in Christian theology the Holy Spirit of God, who is one with the divine principle or the 'Father' and one with the divine Self-Expression or the 'Word' or *Logos* or Eternal Son. With 'them', 'in unity of Godhead', he is to be 'worshipped and adored' by all men. Hence all three *hypostases*, or as we are accustomed to say (and with no great theological accuracy, in view of the specific modern meaning of the word) 'persons', are involved. In this establishment for man, the frustrated and twisted lover, of his capacity to be that for which he is created and which is the true meaning of his life, God is at work. So man is enabled to become a lover, free to love and to receive love, and thus to be fulfilled in love and in loving.

Man, in the Christian understanding, is a dependent creature, who neither caused himself nor explains himself. He depends upon family, friends, environment, food and shelter, historical development in the past, the geography in which that history is set . . . and upon innumerable other factors. All these are the surrogates or representations of his supreme dependence, which is upon God the eternal principle of creativity. Furthermore, man is made in community, so that he cannot live *of* and *to* and *for* himself; he requires his brethren and is knit together with them, as the Old Testament tells us, 'in one bundle of life'. He is neither a body nor a soul; he is body-soul, soul-body, in an organic and total unity in which the body has its rational, affectional, evaluational aspect, while that aspect is itself grounded in and conditioned by his physiological and material body. And man is a sexual being, his total organism equipped for and expressing itself in what Freud taught us to call 'genital' ways, although his sexuality can also be expressed 'anally' and 'orally' as he moves along the path to full 'genitality'. He is possessed of the physiological organs for total human sexual expression, with the accompanying biological drives, emotional desires, and imaginative powers.

In all this man is an unfulfilled capacity. He requires for his completion or self-realization the satisfaction of his basic 'subjective aim'. I use here the language of process-theology which in these and in so many other ways I find especially helpful for Christian thought. That aim or goal of human life is that each man become an agent for the creation of good, in community with his brethren, and in the cosmic order where he is placed. St Augustine's great words, 'Thou hast made us towards thee, O God, and our heart is in disquietude until it finds its rest in thee', stand as the classical statement of this truth about man, who can fulfil his subjective aim and find his satisfaction only when he is in such a relationship with God that it can be said that 'God dwells in him and he in God'.

To say this is to say in other words what is meant when we assert that man's only satisfaction, in the last resort, is to be 'in love' – for 'God is Love'. Thus in all human striving to love and to receive love, in all human sexuality *even when* it is distorted and twisted and frustrated, there is a working of God. The nasty-minded, the super-sophisticated, the over-moralistic, do not see this. Their failure to see it amounts to that condition for which Jesus, in the Fourth Gospel, con-condemned the Pharisees; they are self-blinded. We might put it this way: Love has come into the world, Love is present with us, Love is available for us, and we simply do not wish to recognize its presence, because it somehow offends our delicate sensitivity. We wish to be 'more spiritual', shall we say, than God himself. But we are wrong. And Father Smith, in Bruce Marshall's striking novel *The World, the Flesh, and Father Smith*, was right and Christian when he said that even the man who rings the doorbell of a brothel is 'seeking God'. He is seeking God in the wrong way, of course. He is doing that which will harm rather than help both himself and the women to whom he resorts. But none the less it is *God* whom he is seeking. For what he is seeking in that distorted way is Love – although it appears to him under the dreadfully twisted form of sheer sensuality. But I shall not develop this theme, based as it is on the Christian assurance that *nothing* is evil in itself. To do so would take us too far afield. In any event, I think that a Christian who after deep thought and meditation does *not* see what I am driving at, is in need of no further argument but rather of conversion to the faith which he professes with his lips but does not genuinely accept and believe in his heart and with his mind.

I turn now to speak of some of the characteristics of love in its deepest and truest sense. I should list these as: commitment, mutuality in giving and receiving, genuine tenderness in relationships, intention of faithfulness, 'eager expectancy' (as von Hügel put it) or hopefulness, and the urgent desire for union with another life or with other lives in as complete and full a sense as is possible for man. Let me say something, however briefly, about each of these characteristics.

First, there is *commitment*. By this I mean that love requires that one gives oneself in free dedication to another, so that the lover no longer thinks that he belongs to himself. He is so surrendered to the beloved that his existence finds a new centre in that other. This does *not* suggest a sort of suicidal act in which one attempts to destroy oneself. On the contrary, it is a commitment such as shall establish precisely what our next characteristic points to. This is *mutuality in giving and receiving*. As each of the lovers commits himself to the other, each also finds himself in the other. The relationship between them brings about such a sharing of life, such a participation in each by the other, that they have become in intention and in principle one life which is inclusive of them both. There is interpenetration here, to as full an extent as possible. But such mutuality, or giving and receiving, is in *tenderness*, our third characteristic.

No coercion, no force, no undue and improper pressure, no over-riding of one person by another, can occur in real love. The relationship is of persuasion, in which each besets the other round with his concern and care, and in which the acts of each are gently, graciously and unselfishly performed – whether these be specifically sexual or more generally personal. There is no place in love for sadism, any more than there is a place for masochism. Both of them, suggesting as they do cruel coercion on the one hand or self-inflicted pain on the other, are a distortion of love and a denial of its basic meaning. Again, love is *faithful*, in that it intends to remain with and for the one loved 'until death us do part' – and even beyond death, for there is a quality of eternality about the loving relationship which denies that death can end the faithful commitment which it involves.

Love is also *hopeful*. The lover always looks for and seeks to make possible the best in the beloved, sensing that great truth of which G. M. Hopkins once wrote: 'There lives the dearest freshness deep down things.' He is expectant that the one to whom he is committed in mutual giving and receiving, with tenderness and in faith, will himself have that sort of freshness which will relieve the relationship from being tedious and dull and give it what cynics (speaking more wisely than they know) sometimes call the 'romantic glow'. Finally, love *always seeks union*. But this is not a 'merging' nor the sort of fusion in which each life loses something of its own identity or freedom. That would not be *union* at all, since true union requires that more than one shall be participant in the relationship.

As readers perhaps will have noted, from one point of view all the earlier characteristics are variations on the single theme of *union*. From another point of view, they are all of them aspects of the fulfilment of human personality in community, as personality finds integration in the giving of self and the receiving of self which constitutes true union for men. In securing this union, love always *personalizes* those who share it. The lover is a self in movement towards

D

integration; at the same time, he is related to others. It is this which distinguishes personhood from sheer individuality. An individual is *one* of a given kind, *an instance* of the species manhood. But a person is one who is also open to others, sharing in their lives, affected and influenced by them. He is no 'island entire unto himself'. In loving and being loved we *become* persons; and this occurs precisely because in loving and being loved we are acting *as* and being treated *as* persons. The lover 'wants' another *person:* and he wants another *person* to 'want' him.

One of the most striking illustrations of what I have just been saying is found in an incident in the novel *Giovanni's Room* by the American novelist James Baldwin. This novel portrays two homosexuals, one the American student David, the other the Italian youth Giovanni, with an American girl playing her part as a counterfoil for David's attraction to Giovanni. The scene which beautifully shows the personalizing aspect of love occurs when after a disagreement David finally decides to do what he has been planning for some time – to leave 'Giovanni's room' and so to leave Giovanni. He hurls at Giovanni the charge that it was the physical relationship alone that Giovanni wanted: 'I know *what* you want'. To which Giovanni replies that for him it is not *what* he wanted that matters, it is *who* he wanted. Love, whenever it is real and deep and true, is always in terms of 'who', never 'what' alone.

It may be said by some readers that this chapter has been altogether too ideal. It has painted a picture of love, they will say, that is not in fact realized in ordinary human beings. I am very ready to admit that such is the case. I have insisted that man *is* a sinner. The discussion in the next chapter will be concerned with that unlovely fact. Here, however, I must insist that what I have described is the *direction* in which love always moves. The fullness of commitment, the mutuality in giving and receiving, the tenderness, the faithfulness and hopefulness, the realization of union, and through all these the fulfilment of human

existence in the deepest satisfaction of each man's subjective aim in community with his fellows – yes, these may
not often be, and certainly are not always, attained. Yet
there are more than slight intimations of them in the most
run-of-the mill instances of loving relationship. Every man
seeks, however wrongly, to give himself to another self who
also gives. Every man knows something of these things.
It is towards their complete expression that he is *really*
moving, often enough without being conscious of the fact.

To be on the way to love, in the sense in which I have
sought to describe it, constitutes (I believe) man's distinctive
quality. And to be on the way to such love is to begin to
live, in the most profound sense of that verb. Robert South-
well, the recusant poet, has a lovely sentence saying exactly
this: 'Not where I breathe, but where I love, I live.'

Note The treatment of human nature and of love briefly
presented in this chapter has been developed more fully in
two books by the author: *The Christian Understanding of
Human Nature* (Nisbet, 1964) and *Love Looks Deep* (A. R.
Mowbray & Company, Oxford, 1969).

4

THE MEANING OF SIN

The word 'sin' is one of the most misused and misunderstood words in the religious vocabulary. Its meaning seems to vary with the theologians who use it; and this means, of course, with the particular sort of theological orientation which each of these theologians exhibits. The consequence is a quite enormous confusion. It is not only that theologians themselves are likely to be confused about the word; what is much more important is that ordinary men and women, even when quite devout and well-instructed Christians, share in the confusion.

Let me illustrate this from my own experience. If anyone should be able to grasp the meaning of the concept of sin in Christian thought and experience, it should be the young men who come to a theological college to study for the ministry of the church. After all, these young men have had an intimate acquaintance with Christian faith; doubtless they have done more reading and thinking about it than the average lay person. Yet after teaching theological students for more than a third of a century, I can testify that they are in no better case than others. When they come up to college they sometimes think of sin as a violation of law, both human and divine. Or they think of sin as an offence against the arbitrary fiat of a God who from Mt Sinai gave a set of commandments, the following of which was a guarantee of heaven and disobedience to which was to be punished in hell. Or they think of sin as nothing other than human selfishness seen in religious contexts. Or they think of it as the variety of pride which suggests that its opposite for them is a Uriah Heep mentality requiring them to become (as a friend of mine once put it) 'doormats for others to walk on'. Or – and it is surprising how frequently this is the case – they think of sin as sexual expression, sexual activity, and even sexual desire.

Their notions of sin are only reflections of what they have picked up somewhere; alas, one fears, very often from parish priests or other advisers, or perhaps from taking at face value much that is found in liturgical formulae, in bits of Holy Scripture read out of context, or in sermons and addresses by dignitaries of the church who have been engaging in the popular sport of many religious leaders: decrying the 'sinfulness of our times'.

In a relatively short chapter of a short book, it would be impossible to outline with any adequacy a view of the meaning of sin which is faithful to the important strands in our Christian tradition and at the same time intelligible today. All I can hope to do is offer some suggestions which will help us in our main intention: to see whether, or in what sense, the physical sexual contacts which homosexuals almost inevitably will practise can be called sinful.

The first thing that I should like to emphasize is that we make a great mistake if we define sin simply in terms of overt actions. For a Christian this should be obvious, since we all know that Jesus Christ put his main stress on the *intention* with which an action was performed, the *inner spirit* of the man who performed it, or what we might describe as the *basic attitude* of the person involved. To say this clears away a good deal of misunderstanding, although we should freely acknowledge that much of the conventional moral teaching of the church has been responsible for that misunderstanding. It is true, of course, that some overt acts are evil, because they damage other persons and create situations where only bad consequences can follow. In the traditional moral theology of the church, such actions are called 'material sin'; but that theology also knows that 'formal sin'

– which is to say, the intention of the person doing the act – is much more important.

Having made that point, I must now attempt to distinguish between sin, in the *singular*, and sins, in the *plural*. *Sin* is generally regarded in Christian thought as a state or condition; it is the 'separation' or 'alienation' from God in which men are supposed to be. This state is said to be due to the 'first sin' of Adam which has put all of his descendants in the position of being members of a race deprived of free and open communion with its Creator. The opposite of sin, in this sense, is the 'state of grace', in which the separation or alienation or deprivation has been overcome by God's act and men are once again related to him and openly in the fellowship of sons with their Father. And in general Christian thought *sins* are the *particular* wrong-doings, wrong-speakings, wrong-thinkings, which men in that state perform in one way or another. These sins are both the consequence of human alienation from God and the intentional actions which involve responsibility and guilt on the part of the person who does them.

A good deal of this scheme ought to be seen by modern Christians to rest upon what we now know is an error. That is, it comes from taking as historical fact the biblical stories found in Genesis about the so-called 'Fall of Man' through Adam's specific act of sinning. Far too many theologians today are guilty of the peculiar contradiction of admitting (on the one hand) that the biblical material here is highly mythological and dependent upon ancient legends which have no claim to be regarded as historical, yet (on the other hand) treating this material, for theological purposes, as if it *were* historical. This is theological double-talk for which there is no justification whatsoever. What the stories are concerned to do, so far as we can get their point, is to present in the form of 'tales' the deeply felt experience of men and women who knew themselves to be alienated from God. Yet even this statement requires a certain amount of qualification. For the alienation of which we speak does not mean that there is nothing of God left to men, no contact with him whatsoever, no sort of communion or fellowship with God which all men possess whether or not they are conscious of the fact. Rather, it means – or ought to be taken to mean – that man has a *broken* or *damaged* relationship with God. There is not a constant openness on his part to the insistent loving pressure of the divine reality upon him. Yet man is not 'totally depraved', no matter what some famous Christian thinkers have said. To talk of him in that fashion is really to blaspheme, for it entails either the view that God's creation is not good or that God is so impotent that he has let it get out of his hands and beyond his control. In the main Christian tradition it is never forgotten that man is *still* made in 'the image of God', however much he may have damaged 'the likeness of God' in him.

The position stated in the last sentence is essentially that of St Irenaeus, when he distinguished in Genesis 1.26 between 'image' and 'likeness'. Modern biblical scholars as well as the great continental reformers have correctly pointed out that St Irenaeus is here guilty of faulty exegesis of a particular biblical text. But faulty exegesis sometimes can be the expression of profound penetration into the *general* trend of biblical thought. Unless we are biblical fundamentalists, the precise letter of a text is not so important as the meaning which it can be seen to possess in the total biblical pattern as the enlightened Christian reads and interprets it. Obviously the original text is employing Hebrew parallelism: 'image' and 'likeness' meant the same thing to the writer of that text. But the general presupposition about the *sense* of the biblical view, which St Irenaeus entertained when he approached this text, made it possible for him to discern the distinction between man as God creates him and intends him to be, on the one hand, and the concrete situation in respect to man's realization of that creative intention, on the other.

Thus we may say that the truth is exactly that which in our last chapter we were attempting to state. Man is made by God to be a lover; but in actual fact, he is a frustrated lover, whose loving is distorted or twisted. In other words, man's state or condition is the state or condition of one who is inhibited in the full expression of his love and who in the concrete and particular expressions of his love misdirects it or attaches it to objects which are unworthy of this concentration of desire. It is those concrete and particular expressions which constitute man's *sins*, just as it is the frustration of his loving and his present inability to order that loving aright which is his *sin*, in the more general sense of the term.

The frustration of man as lover is not *in itself* a sinful state, although since it is not what God wants for man it might be called a state that is objectively wrong. For myself, however, I wish that we would not talk this way, although it is possible to do so, and perhaps to some people, highly attractive. For we must remember that man's frustration is to a large degree the result of his being a finite creature, who in his finitude is not able to be or to do all that he has it in him to be or do. His historical situation, his geographical location, his environment, and many other factors, for which he is not responsible in any sense, enter in here. But the inability to order his loving *aright* is in a somewhat different category. In that inability man is to a considerable degree the victim of his inheritance. The many loveless acts of men and women in the past (if one can speak of any act as being *totally* loveless, which I doubt in the light of all that modern psychology has taught us), the accumulation of wrong choices, the environing conditions which a man accepts without protest, as well as the decisions that he himself has made in years or days or even minutes gone by, have all had their part in creating the kind of inability to which I refer. His deep memory and his present relationships are a very real part of the picture; these constitute the material with which that other and particularly identifying factor – the subjective aim which has been chosen or accepted and which is on the way to being realized – has to deal.

I should wish to claim that it is in respect to the desire or urge towards the satisfaction of aim – the integrating purpose in each human life – that the distorting or twisting in our human loving becomes a matter of our own personal responsibility. This is only another and long-winded way of saying exactly what Jesus taught; it is the *spirit* of the inner man, as he makes his decisions, that produces *sins*, meaning his *specific actions* in thought, word, or deed.

In this inner spirit, where man decides on ways of using his memory and his present relationships, including everything that goes to make up and to surround him, for the satisfaction of what he has chosen to be his *aim*, we find the root difficulty in our human loving. Nor is this a matter of sheer individualism. Our belonging with our fellows in the one 'bundle of life' has its part in establishing man for what he is, as well as in the results of each and every decision he makes. The whole of man is involved here, too, since this inner spirit is not merely temporary resident in a physical body but is that aspect of the total man which is possessed of the ability – however limited in extent this may be – to make precisely such decisions towards satisfying his aim.

But man is a dynamic personality, much more on the way to becoming himself than an actualized self in the full and complete sense. Thus he is always to be understood as *moving towards* fulfilment. When he twists or distorts his loving, he is damaging the personality which he is on the way to becoming; he is then moving towards less than his proper and complete fulfilment. This is possible for him since he has sufficient freedom to make significant choices that effect the movement towards fulfilment. He is at liberty to centre his energies on the kind of fulfilment which is not for his own best good and not for the best good of the community of men of which he is a part.

I have spoken several times about man's relationships. All our actions are intimately tied in with those relationships. Whatever we do or say or think, however individual to ourselves it may seem to be at the moment, it can only be understood in its true depth when we see its tremendous effect on *others*. Since we are not 'islands entire unto ourselves' but are 'part of the continent' (in familiar phrases from John Donne, one of which we have previously quoted), we do not and we cannot act as if only ourselves were involved in our action. When we think we are doing this, we are only fooling ourselves. The whole cosmos is affected by what we do, whether or not we are aware of this. More immediately, the persons with whom we are related in more intimate ways, the neighbours who are close to us, and through them others of our race, are affected by our actions. And let us remember that our *actions* always rest upon that inner spirit which is each man's decision to satisfy his subjective aim in this or that particular way and at this or that particular time.

Now we must ask the specifically 'religious' question: what is God's will for man? We can say at once that it is not arbitrarily imposed upon his creatures, as if some oriental despot handed down regulations which bore no relation to, any more than he himself had any concern for, his subjects. God's will for man is that *man shall be man*; or as Dr Paul Lehmann in his book *Ethics in a Christian Context* has so well stated it, God's will for man is that *he shall be human and remain human*. God's purpose or will is adapted to the nature which is ours as his creatures, in whatever sense we may wish to understand God's creation of the world and of men in that world.

Morality in the Christian sense simply *cannot* be, what so often it has been taken to be, a description of some set of divine laws or rules which must be accepted and followed without deviation just because they are *imposed* upon us. That is not the way in which God works; and it is one of the tragedies of Christian theology that instead of taking what Whitehead called 'the Galilean vision' as its model for God's nature and his agency in the world, it has all too often prefered Caesar in his majesty, the despot in his autocratic, concern, or 'the ruthless moralist' whose only interest is in telling people what to do and then punishing them because they obey him. God's way of working in his world is by his unfailing persuasion and his lure, the love 'which will not let us go'. By these means he labours unceasingly, with inexhaustible resources at his command, to bring the creation to the fullness of the possibilities which he has planted in it. In the terms of the process-philosophy which I myself accept he provides the 'initial subjective aim' for each creature, its basic purpose. He works without rest yet without haste in order that this initial aim may by free acceptance and decision become the aim of each creature. He surrounds and penetrates every entity or occasion in the world with his creative and never-failing love, that it may be brought to the fullest possible degree of satisfaction. The aim is first God's; then it is the aim which the creature has freely taken for its own.

There are two remarks which I must interpolate here. One is that what I have just been saying is no soft, easy, sentimental, and 'sloppy' view of God and his dealings with us. Far from it. It is starkly realistic and it suggests that love is altogether stronger and more effective than most of us have ever dared or cared to think. Love is 'stronger than an army with banners'; it is the only really strong thing in the world. It is also more effective than coercion or force, for these can secure only unwilling, grudging, and resentful acceptance, whereas love can win from the loved one the free, full, and glad response which, as our Lord himself has told us, is the occasion for 'joy in heaven'.

The second remark which I here interpolate is that this view makes *demands* upon men. It does not simply acquiesce in their lethargy, not to speak of their distortion and twisting in loving. In a world which is 'on the move', great aims are in view. Each man is given the chance to co-operate, as what Whitehead ventured to call 'a co-creator with God', in the making of good in all its manifestations and with all its marvellous diversity and glory. Some of my readers may be familiar with the story about Crillon, in the Hundred Years War. While his comrades were engaged in the battle at Arques, he remained behind, sulking in his tent. The commander came upon him after the battle and shouted to him,

'Hang yourself, brave Crillon, *we* fought at Arques and *you* were not there.' That puts my point precisely.

In this great movement of a processive universe towards the good which God purposes for it and works to establish in it, men are given their place and part. If they refuse that offer, they are self-condemned. No divine judgement in some external fashion need be imposed upon them, for they 'go to their own place' precisely in their rejection of the invitation. They are called to be lovers, ordering their loving aright in the light of the love which is *God's* Love in action; and of every son of man it can be affirmed that he will be appraised in *those* terms. St John of the Cross once wrote, 'In the evening of our day, we shall be judged by our loving'. Need more be said, to those who claim to be Christians and whose life is 'in Christ', which is to say, whose life is in the Love declared and enacted in the man Jesus who is now regnant as Love triumphant over all sinning, all evil, and even over death itself?

Let us now attempt to relate what has been said in *this* chapter to the Christian view of human nature which was outlined in the last one.

First of all, it is apparent that human sin is seen when we seek to live in the denial of our dependence upon God and upon others. It is seen when we live as if we were simply animals, turning our human existence into something more suited for the barnyard than for the community of men. Equally, it is seen when we pretend to be 'disembodied spirits', as if we were without bodies; for this is to commit the sin which Jacques Maritain once called 'angelism', the effort to deny our embodied status and live *as if* we were 'angels' arrogantly claiming for ourselves that which is not ours. It is seen when we deny our relationships with, and our utter need of, other men, in the human community of which we are a part, when we attempt to live in 'rugged individualism' which disregards others and seek only our own interests. It is seen when we let our human sexuality become warped and ingrown, stamping down our sexual nature or denying the goodness of human sex in order to compensate for some frustration or disappointment which has come upon us.

So much for the *general* pattern of our manhood. When it comes to our loving, that for which we were made and which is the dynamic drive and the deep desire of human existence, the same sort of thing can be said. When we decline all commitment and attempt to live with no concern for some over-arching and dominant purpose, we are living without true love. When we refuse mutuality, so that in our relationships we seek only to 'get' but not to give or we refuse to receive from others that which they can give us and which they urgently desire to give us, we are living without true love. When we exert coercive pressure on others and thus endeavour to force them to our way of thinking or acting; and when we fail to be tender in our relationship with them, we are not living in true love. When we have no intention of loyalty or when we consistently reject the claims to faithfulness, we are not living in true love. When we take towards others the attitude of exploitation and hence 'use' them for our own ends without regard to their desires; or when we take towards them the attitude of exploration, regarding others as interesting specimens to be studied and dissected and observed as if they were biological specimens in a laboratory, we are not living truly in love. Hopefulness, or expectation in respect to that which others have it in them to be, is lacking in us. When we seek to avoid all deep union with others, and are ready to have only superficial and undemanding relationships with them, making it easy for ourselves to avoid the purification of self which genuine union always demands and always effects, we are living without true love.

From what has just been said, it will be apparent that most of us much of the time, and all of us some of the time, are sinners. We rightly say, 'This is too high; I cannot attain unto it'. Of course that is true. But the question is, not what we are *now*, but in what *direction we are moving*. If man were a static entity, then we might well be in despair. But we are processive creatures, *becoming* men, *on the way* to the realization of our personhood, *moving towards* the satisfaction of our aim, not yet fulfilled but *going towards* fulfilment. Hence we have no reason for dispair. In any event, such despair is unchristian. *God* is with us; *his* Love surrounds us; *his* call still summons us. These homiletic clichés are much more than conventional material found in a sermon or devotional address. They are practical reality.

The gospel of God in Jesus Christ gives us the assurance that no matter what may be our state of frustration or our impotence in loving or our distortions and our twistings, 'he that is with us is greater than (anything) that can be against us'. In the correct translation of his usually mistranslated passage in Romans 8.28, St Paul tells us that 'God works towards a good end, and in every respect, for those who love him'. When our human loving is seen as mysteriously participant in the divine love, things look different from the deadness and drabness of existence where the divine vision is lacking.

We men cannot fly to God, extricating ourselves from the 'changes and chances of this mortal life'; we must find him here and now in our concrete human experience or we shall never find him at all. Yet as St Augustine has told us, we do not need to climb to the heavens to find the way in which we can live in love. 'The way has come to us; let us walk in it', he says. Jesus Christ, for Christian faith, *is* the way of love; he is the cosmic Love personified. In him the cosmic Lover is made available to our eyes and ears, and to our hearts and wills as well, in a degree and manner unprecedented and unparalleled.

When I began that last paragraph I intended to continue with a further development of its theme. But I shall not do so. I shall ask the reader to do something for himself. Let him take his New Testament and turn to the First Epistle of St John; in that Epistle let him open to the fourth chapter. Let him then read that chapter slowly, carefully, and prayerfully. Everything that I should have wished to say is there, and with a directness and immediacy that I should be a fool to attempt to imitate. Whoever wrote that Epistle knew what he was talking about as a Christian. He may not have been the disciple who was so close to Jesus that it was said of him that he was 'the disciple whom Jesus loved'. Almost certainly he was not that disciple. But none the less he knew the Lord Jesus as the Love which he had seen and touched and handled; he knew what it means to live 'in Christ', although he does not use that Pauline phrase. He *knew*.

When *we* talk about sin, we must never let that kind of knowledge fall into the background. It is only in the context of our knowledge of love – love of God in the brethren, love of the brethren in God – that we can speak about ourselves as sinners. We *are* sinners; but we are also 'the dear children of God's love'. If we permit God's love, and the Love which *is* God, to become central in our thought, we shall indeed understand ourselves as sinners. What is much more important, we shall understand God's will for us and we shall be remarkably engraced for the doing of it.

5

THE HOMOSEXUAL CONDITION AND HOMOSEXUAL ACTS

It may be useful to note at the outset that the word 'homosexual' does *not* mean as many people seem to think, 'sexually inclined towards a man'. The word is a barbarous compound from Greek and Latin roots: *homo* in Greek meaning 'the same'; *sexual* from Latin needing no translation. A homosexual is a person who loves members of his *own* sex or wishes to 'have sex' with them and with them only. This is the basic meaning of the homosexual *condition*. A homosexual person may be male or female; he is a person who wishes to love and can only love, in the most complete and intimate sense of that verb with its physical overtones and suggestions, another person of his or her own sex. That is the way he *is*; that is his state or condition.

This helps us to understand why it is that whereas a heterosexual man, for example, will find delight in looking at and admiring the beauty or charm of a woman, the homosexual male will find *his* delight in looking at and admiring a man. To him the male, not the female, is beautiful, although of course homosexuals will not disdain feminine beauty or attractiveness. For a woman who is homosexual, it is another woman who is attractive, although she may also like men and enjoy their companionship as friends. At this point it may be well also to notice that many male homosexuals very often like women and enjoy their company. A considerable number of women, I am told, return the compliment; and it is said, with what justice I do not know for I have never sought to enquire, that this liking which women often have for homosexual men, and men for lesbians, is because in their company they feel that they are being taken as human beings, rather than as possible sexual partners. However that may be, it is certainly true that male homosexuals often like to be with women, to dine with them, to accompany them to the theatre, to converse with them – and similarly with homosexual women and male friends.

Nor is this because the typical homosexual male is himself a rather feminine type. For the most part, so far as observation tells us, he is entirely masculine in appearance and in manner. There *are* the others, of course; in Italy these are called, appropriately enough, *femminili*. Such men sometimes dress and often act like members of the female sex; they assume what they take to be feminine 'airs' and they emulate feminine ways of speaking and behaving. I do not wish to condemn such men; doubtless there are reasons, maybe good reasons, for this assumed feminity. But I am confident that the majority of homosexual men not only do not resemble them, but find them objectionable. They may not, probably would not, indulge in too severe criticism, since they are well aware of the fact that men of this sort are part of the total homosexual picture; yet they do not wish to be seen with them too much and often they try to avoid going to parties or other meetings where the *femminili* may predominate. In a similar way, homosexual females often dislike the very 'butch' or masculine type of woman – and most of them are very obviously feminine and do not ape the male sex.

Of the male homosexuals whom I myself have known – and here I am sure that my own experience is entirely like that of most other people – there have been only one or two who have been in any sense feminine in manner or attitude or external behaviour. Most of those I know have been quite different from this. They have been masculine, sometimes almost excessively so. Some of them have been of the muscular, athletic sort, who play games with vigour, who indulge in body-building, and who pride themselves on their physical strength. Their tastes and interests have been equally

E

masculine. Indeed, to any observer who did not know their particular sexual inclination, they would seem very much like any other man whom one might meet. This is part of what I meant to indicate in the first chapter when I remarked that a homosexual may just as well be a bank director or a lorry-driver. It is said by some who have a wide acquaintance with homosexual men that as a matter of fact, the majority are sturdy 'he-men' (in the American vulgarism), quite likely to be engaged in a job requiring physical strength. One of my correspondents, speaking of his own pastoral contacts with such men, has said that many of those whom he has tried to help have been from the building-trades, from areas of artisanry which demand considerable resistance to hard and exacting work, and with duties that call forth considerable courage in face of danger.

One thing, however, seems true of almost all homosexuals: they are in certain important ways sensitive and gentle people. A psychiatrist has told me that he is convinced that *on the whole* homosexuals are more sensitive than their heterosexual brothers and sisters. I do not know whether this is the case as a general rule; yet the men with whom I have had to do, mostly young men in their late 'teens' or in their 'twenties', have seemed to me to show just such sensitivity. They have also had a certain gentleness once one got beneath what seemed on the surface to be a kind of compensatory aggressiveness in conversation about their homosexual condition. It may very well be the case that an excess of that gentleness in certain men produces in them the feminine manners and actions to which I have referred. And it is quite likely that the sensitivity which one observes and which my psychiatrist friend found so striking is the explanation of the common and mistaken belief that homosexuals are all 'arty' even when they are not professional artists.

The Quaker Report on sexuality has spoken of the marked interest of many male homosexuals in the body and especially in the sexual member of the body. It has noted what it calls a certain 'phallic' centring of attention. I believe that this is true of *male* homosexuals, although a similar interest does not appear to be present in lesbians. It gives some explanation for the fascination which some men of this type show for sculptures of naked men, and why photographs such as those published in some of the homosexual publications have their peculiar appeal. One American writer has also said that a considerable number of male homosexuals are possessed by what he calls 'the mystique of the large penis'. By this he means that they delight in looking at men who are 'equipped', so to say, in this fashion; and that in their phantasies, they often dwell on such matters. I do not know how accurate his observation may be; but I believe that there can be no question about the Quaker Report's comment on 'phallic' interest. Some may find this very unpleasant; but it is difficult to see why it is any *more* unpleasant than the voyeur of heterosexual tastes, who is sometimes exceedingly offensive, especially to the women who are the victims of his glances.

It is not really very helpful to concentrate attention on this sort of manifestation, although it was necessary to mention it. It is much better to consider the desire of the homosexual to find a loving relationship with another of his own sex. If what I have said about human nature and especially about human love is correct, the need to give oneself to another who gives in return is so deep in our common humanity that it is not surprising that the homosexual shares it too. It would be incredible if he did not. What he is seeking is *love*; in this respect he is like all human beings. I do not mean simply love which is given to him, I mean also love which he can give. Like others, the homosexual yearns to be in a relationship of commitment, mutuality in giving and receiving, tenderness, loyalty, expectancy, and union. Deep within himself he knows that this alone will bring him fulfilment or what I have styled the satisfaction of his basic and identifying subjective aim. Being what he is, the only fashion in which he is able to achieve this fulfilment, and the only way in which he is able to envisage its possibility, is with another person of his own sex. The desire to find precisely such a relationship is so much a part of him that he cannot escape it if he would.

We shall do well to recognize that very few human beings are called to a celibate life. Those who are thus called may find in religious communities ways of answering the call by becoming 'religious' in the technical sense. They may become monks or nuns. Others may find that the particular work which they feel obliged to undertake demands that they eschew all physical sexual contacts. It would be a grave injustice to such persons to think of them as *a*-sexual. They have succeeded in channelling their sexual desires and drives in such a fashion that these are used, directed, and satisfied in other ways – perhaps by utter concentration on the love of God, or by the service of their fellow-men, or by some particular cause or object or even person which takes all there is of them and in which they find their delight and satisfaction. There are still other men and women who through no choice of their own have been obliged to live in a celibate fashion. They may let this necessity warp them so that they become ingrown and disagreeable. But this need not be the case. All of us have known men and women who, by accepting necessity in such fashion that fate becomes destiny, have been able to remain sweet and wholesome, perhaps even to become more sweet and wholesome than otherwise they might have been.

Yet it is apparent that this kind of vocation or this sort of acceptance is not possible for the great majority of human beings. For most of us the expression of our created nature as lovers will be by loving another person; and with this there will go the desire for the sexual expression of love in physical contacts of various kinds. Here once again, the homosexual is no different from others, save in the sex of the person he loves. He too yearns for another to whom he may give himself; he too yearns for another who will give himself to him. There is nothing sinful or wicked in this; it is as natural as it is for a man to be human.

Some men are prepared to say, in respect to the homosexual's yearning which finds its only possible satisfaction in another man or woman, 'Well, what of it? What difference does it make?' Of course it *does* make some difference, if for no other reason than that society at present is likely to condemn or, if not to condemn, to sympathize in the wrong way. 'Poor chap, or poor girl, I know he or she is made that way, but it is really too bad. They are "sick" and we must put up with them in their "sickness". But of course they are not quite normal and are to be pitied.' For the homosexual this attitude is sometimes more difficult to accept than outright condemnation; nobody likes to be 'pitied' in that way, especially if he himself has no reason whatever to think that he is 'sick'. So far as he can see, he is acting in accordance with his deepest instincts and his most profound impulses; he is behaving according to the 'nature' which somehow has been given him. He is not *seeking* to pervert anyone, to seduce anyone, to 'buy love' (save as society forces him to do so), or to be promiscuous with one partner after another. What he *is* seeking is to give himself to another human being and to receive from another human being the same quality of love as that which he is anxious to give.

To be quite frank here, I find it difficult not to be indignant at the people who lack understanding of the deepest drives in others but are quite ready to demand recognition of such drives in themselves. I am indignant at those who can only sneer or condemn, or pity and sigh, or (worst of all, perhaps) laugh indulgently, at such 'odd' behaviour and such 'queer' desires. And my indignation can turn almost to fury towards those condemning persons, pitying persons, amused persons. Have they no compassion, no fellow-feeling with others, no capacity to grasp the plain fact that everyone is not like themselves? Fortunately, church leaders, moral theologians, and many others who speak for organized religion have the grace these days to avoid such attitudes. They are prepared to acknowledge, however reluctantly some of them seem to do it, that the homosexual state is *not* sinful; that the homosexual cannot help himself in this situation; and that common charity requires that we shall accept him as he is and in the way he is.

As we said earlier, most informed people nowadays would not *condemn* the homosexual for being what he is, nor if they are Christians would they refuse him the Christian acceptance given to any man who seeks to join with them in the community of faith. The lot of the homosexual is easier these days, because he knows that the fact of his homosexual condition does not of itself prevent him from being regarded and treated as a human being. Yet it still remains true that if he *is* to be accepted, he is expected by religious leaders to refrain from any acts which give external expression to his impulses. In other words, the demand is made that he shall be a celibate, although he is in no way conscious of a specific vocation to celibacy. Neither is he one of those who are entirely unable to find another human being with whom they may establish a union in which commitment, mutuality, tenderness, loyalty or faithfulness, hopefulness, true union of lives, with the resulting satisfaction of subjective aim in personal fulfilment, will be present.

The attitude which demands of the homosexual no physical expression of his love, seems to me inhuman, unjust, and above all unchristian. I do not understand it nor can I find any reason to support it. I shall argue the point in a following chapter. In the present context, I can say only that many of us who have been given the opportunity to know and talk with homosexuals are scandalized by what seems to be worse than a failure to understand; in fact, what seems to be close to hypocrisy.

As I have been writing the last few pages, my mind has turned continually to a man who is well-known to me but will not be known to my readers and to whom therefore I may refer without any violation of confidence. He is reasonably attractive, intelligent, highly successful in his work. In terms of the things which the world esteems he is a person to be envied, for he has made his mark and has been accepted as an authority in his chosen field. He is a professional man, but he might just as well be a lorry-driver, a teacher, a doctor, a business executive, or anything else. For far too many years – or so it seemed to him – he had sought to trample on what he knew perfectly well were his real desires. He had even endeavoured to become entirely celibate, although not a 'religious', for he felt no vocation to that life. He was a Christian, regular in his observance and genuinely convinced in his Christian faith.

But something was always lacking. He knew that he needed a kind of fulfilment which he had not yet found; the lack of it was a gnawing pain and a continuing emptiness in his life. Then, one day, he met another man. In the phrase we commonly use about heterosexuals, he 'fell in love' and the other man 'fell in love' with him. They saw much of each other; they spent a holiday together; and they found that in a remarkable way each was the complement of the other. They were most surely committed to each other; they knew the mutuality of giving and receiving; they were tender one with the other; they vowed, not in word but in intention, true loyalty. Each of them had a deep expectation of what the other might come to be. They were in the most profound sense united. And each of them experienced the joy which is present in the human movement towards fulfilment. It was almost inevitable that sooner or later they should desire to cement this relationship in physical actions which would express and make even more binding the union which existed between them. They engaged in such acts; in them they found themselves utterly at one, with nothing held back. I came to know that their physical contacts went to what might be described as 'the limit'; but they saw nothing nasty or disgraceful in them, rather they found them a mode of giving and receiving that was to both more than just appropriate. Whenever they engaged in these contacts, it was an occasion of enormous delight and joy.

They were both homosexuals. That was their condition, their state. They knew and accepted the fact of their homosexuality, with all its implications and in full awareness of the attitude which society at large would adopt if the intimacy of their relationship should ever become known. The one whom I knew best was, as I have said, a convinced Christian and a regular communicant; the other was a nominal Christian, perhaps a little more, for he 'practised', as we say, on occasion. Through his friend the latter came to see more and more meaning in Christian faith and in the reality of the love of God in Christ Jesus about which that friend would often speak.

What was a priest, who knew one of them very well, to say about the whole situation? Was he to urge that they abandon physical acts? Was he to demand that they break the relationship, since it was quite clear that if they continued together physical acts were certain to occur? *There* is the question which had to be answered by a worthy, honest, devout, charitable, compassionate clergyman. He was faced with the decision whether to cut these men, and especially one of them, off from the grace which participation in the Christian community provides. The answer which was given was a positive one; he did *not* cut them off nor suggest that they separate. For this I at least am grateful. I concurred with his decision. But would others? Would most priests or ministers, most Christian laymen and laywomen? Here I am trespassing on the subject of a later chapter, so I shall not pursue the matter for the moment.

I must now speak briefly of the kinds of physical contact in which homosexuals like these men engage. Physical contact of the types now to be described, I hope not offensively, are often considered as in and of themselves sinful when performed between men; it is these contacts which, in one degree of importance or another, have long been regarded in most Anglo-Saxon countries as criminal acts which are punishable by law.

First, there is simple physical touch or embrace. Usually this contact has not been regarded too seriously by moral theologians nor has it been thought to be criminal. But the next sort of contact falls into both categories as these have commonly been established. I refer to what is sometimes styled 'full bodily contact'. The partners who are unclothed embrace each other and hold each other close, pressing their bodies together. For some men this in itself is sufficient to produce orgasm with ejaculation.

Then there is the act generally given the name of mutual masturbation. Here each partner stimulates the sexual organ of the other, until climax is reached. Sometimes this is done successively, sometimes simultaneously. Along with this act, although of course sometimes apart from it, may go kissing which may involve penetration of the mouth of one partner by the tongue of the other.

A more intimate sexual contact is *fellatio*. In the bluntest terms, this is the introduction of the penis of one man into the mouth of the other, with such continued licking and sucking of the inserted member that ejaculation is the result. *Fellatio* can also be performed mutually and simultaneously, by placing bodies in such a position that each can receive the penis of the other into his mouth. We are told by those who claim to know that such a practice – either by one partner at a time or by both at the same time – is most popular among North American homosexuals of the male sex, although it is certainly also practised by a large number of men in Britain.

The last kind of contact is one that seems to many persons disgusting and almost inhuman – although we are now aware of its being fairly frequently performed by heterosexuals in their relations with their partners and hence we can no longer dismiss it as abnormal if by this we mean unusual and infrequent. This contact involves the insertion of the penis of one member, made sufficiently rigid to permit such penetration, into the anus of the other; the insertion is usually followed by movements more or less copulatory in nature which have the effect of making the physical relationship not dissimilar to penile-vaginal contact between persons of differing sex. Various positions are possible here, despite the prevalent belief that only entrance from the rear can be accomplished. Homosexuals often find it easy to have a frontal contact, which permits fondling and kissing to accompany the penile insertion and the motions which are made by one within the other. Anal contacts are said – again by sexual experts – to be preferred by British homosexuals and they are popular on the continent of Europe.

So much for male homosexual acts. What about such acts between women? In general there are three ways in which women may engage in physical sexual relations. The first and most obvious is mutual masturbation, with fondling and caressing of the partners' bodies and with special attention to the sexual parts. The second is the female equivalent of *fellatio*; this is *cunnilingus*, which is the use of the tongue for licking or sucking the clitoris of the partner. The third, sometimes known as tribadism, is an attempt to act in a fashion similar to that followed in heterosexual intercourse, with one partner lying on the other in a position where each may stimulate the clitoris of the other. This last is evidently rather infrequent since it requires a considerable amount of practice and is not at all easy to perform to the satisfaction of each partner.

Despite a popular misunderstanding, it would seem that most lesbians do not care to use an artificial penis, in which one partner pretends to be male by wearing such a device and employing it in a heterosexual fashion through insertion into the other. These devices are not unknown, to be sure; very likely some women find their use attractive, but from what one can gather this is not at all general.

As with male acts, the purpose of the female ones is intended, biologically or physiologically speaking, to be the inducing of orgasm in one or both partners. But it must be insisted that the *primary* intention in homosexual lovemaking is much more the establishment of a relationship of intimacy – of love, indeed – with the physical orgasm as part of that pattern. When a man or woman employs a prostitute, the situation is perhaps different; and so also with the occasional promiscuous meeting. But it is my own conviction, based on what evidence I can discover, that even there the *real desire*, answering to the *real need*, is closeness, intimacy, a sense of belonging one to the other; and that the delight in physical acts, with the result in high sexual excitement, is always to be set in *that* context.

According to experts, a good deal of the talk about 'active' and 'passive' homosexuals, whether they be male or female, is very fanciful. It is of course true that in general personality-pattern *some* male homosexuals are very masculine and others feminine in manner, as we have already noted. It is also true that there are masculine-mannered lesbians as well as gentler (hence more 'feminine') ones. But the theory that in such sexual activity as we have mentioned there is an exclusive pattern which follows such supposed types is nowadays regarded as mistaken. A very masculine sort of man may turn out, in actual sexual contacts, to be extremely gentle, and *vice-versa*; so also with women.

Furthermore, extensive questioning of homosexuals about the 'roles' they prefer in such contacts reveals, we are told, that most homosexuals will on occasion play *any* role which is agreeable to them or which they think or know will please their partner. Thus the idea that certain men always and consistently act as the aggressor, so to say, while others always act as the 'recipient' – and similarly with women – is evidently in error. But really this view was wrong from the start in assuming that (on the one hand) a given male homosexual was essentially feminine in manner and interest or (on the other hand) essentially masculine but with a preference to perform what were in effect male actions but enjoyed with another man. In like manner a false assumption was made about lesbians. What the view failed to see is that while homosexuals do not constitute what sometimes has been styled a 'third sex', neither male nor female but something else, they *do* have their own kind of character pattern and they *do* engage in sexual activity according to that pattern, not according to some supposedly dominant male or female pattern as the case may be.

It is to be noted that none of these types of sexual contacts is in itself peculiarly homosexual; all of them are practised by many heterosexuals in their relations with the other sex, although of course some find this or that particular act distasteful or unpleasant and do not wish to engage in it. In at least one sense of the word 'normal' – not in the sense usually employed in traditional ethical discussion where the word means 'in agreement with man's "God-given" nature' – these sexual acts cannot be described as abnormal, since they are so widely practised by persons of both sexes and in relation to persons of both sexes. We shall have something more to say about the traditional meaning of the word in the eighth chapter, when we discuss the question of the morality of homosexual physical contacts.

The male homosexual who finds himself deeply in love with another man is very likely, indeed almost certainly, anxious to engage in some of these actions. To him they appear entirely appropriate and fitting. He does not think of them as 'dirty' or 'nasty'; quite the contrary. For him they are a way in which he can express his love in a physical way. Perhaps we may believe that he should not do this, but the fact is that this is what he wishes to do and what his partner wishes him to do. For the homosexual to want to act in these ways, or in one of them, is natural to him, since only so can he manifest in the fullest way the love which is deepest in his personality. So also with homosexual women.

Let us put it this way. A man who is committed to another, who wishes to have with the other the mutuality which is giving and receiving, who feels tenderness towards the other, who wishes to give himself in faithful and hopeful union with the other, will almost inevitably desire to express this. He will seek an expression which is so total, so much the *whole* of him, that it will include physical contacts of one sort or another. To fail in this last respect, he thinks, would be to hold back something of himself. It would not be the kind of love which is all-inclusive of himself, either as the giver or the recipient.

Obviously such physical stimulation will often mark a first step along the path to full love. But this is equally true of heterosexuals. Physical acts not only express, but they also create, more general or total personal feelings and yearnings. They manifest the desire for union and they also help to bring that union into existence or to increase its intensity. We might say that such acts are both *ex*pressive and *im*pressive. Indeed this is the case with almost all those outward and visible signs which men naturally perform – a handshake not only expresses friendly greeting, but it aids in establishing the friendship of which it is then the 'sacramental' sign. It is absurd to deny either side. The homosexual is no different from others in this respect; all that is different is that in the specifically sexual attraction which he feels for a member of his own sex, he experiences both expression and impression in a way not shared by his heterosexual brother. The latter finds this double reality in contacts with a person of a sex not his own; this is not possible for the homosexual, whose finding of the same reality can only be with one of his own sex.

I repeat here that I am not concerned to defend the promiscuous homosexual nor the one who resorts to prostitutes. But neither am I willing to defend the heterosexual who in his own fashion does the same with persons of the other sex. Nor am I speaking of seduction or coercion into sexual activity. I am talking about what I have styled the 'conscientious' homosexual. *That* sort of homosexual does not really *want* to seek what in the jargon of his 'world' are called 'one-night stands'; neither is he desirous of paying for the services of a person whom he can use for his own physical satisfaction. Very likely a great number of homosexuals feel themselves driven to such promiscuity or to the employment of a prostitute; but that is not the point. The same could be said about many heterosexuals as well. Simple justice demands that we do not confuse the homosexual about whom I am now talking with the mere sensualist, just as it demands that we make a distinction between the conscientious heterosexual and the man who picks up prostitutes or uses 'call-girls' or engages in easy promiscuity with any woman who is 'available' to him and agreeable to his advances.

We have seen that it is conceded these days, by almost all who have given the matter any careful attention, that the homosexual is not to be condemned as sinful simply because he *is* a homosexual. Whatever may have brought him to that condition, the fact in itself is not wicked; it is simply a given fact, to be accepted like any other fact. Some think that homosexuality is congenital – a drive or tendency with which certain persons are born. Others believe that it is the result of a variety of sociological factors which, as it is sometimes put, have 'conditioned' this or that man to be of such a type. Still others put their emphasis on psychological pressures, such as excessive 'mother-love' in early childhood, or unhappy relations with one's father, or unhealthiness in sibling-relations. Nobody seems to *know*; all these accounts are no more than educated guesses based simply on a survey of the particular kind of person with whom the given expert has had dealings.

Whatever may be the genetic account, it is clear enough that *most* homosexuals do not really wish to be otherwise. *Some* of them do, especially of course those who consult psychiatrists and ask to be 'cured'. There seems to be a certain amount of success in these 'cures'; but a reading of reports about them suggests that this occurs only in those cases where for one reason or another the patient himself disliked his condition and desperately desired to be different. In my experience, the ordinary homosexual – even the one who wants to be 'helped' by a pastor or priest – is not asking to be 'cured'. He would not be otherwise than he is, for his degree of satisfaction in love has been obtained only in this fashion. What he does want is to be assisted in making the best of his condition.

This usually means that he wants help in his effort to establish a relationship with another person of his own sex which will have about it those characteristics which we have described as elements in true love. He wants to make *that* relationship as rich and rewarding for both of them as it is possible for it to be. He knows that social pressures are against him and that most of the people whom he meets in his office or shop or school find his kind of sexuality repugnant or at least distasteful. He has been forced to accept this as part of the given situation. But still he wants to do the best that he can and he wishes to have with the person whom he loves a relationship which will be truly committed, in complete mutuality, entirely tender, fully loyal, abounding in hope, and establishing as intimate and satisfying a union as is open to them under these very adverse conditions and in these very difficult surroundings. He is asking a great deal, of course. But it is almost never the strictly *physical* side which worries him; that aspect of the relationship is so inevitable and appropriate, in his eyes, that to think of abandoning or abjuring it would be close to suicide.

But if the state or condition of homosexuality is not sinful, are those physical contacts which we have described to be classified as sin? Here the majority of Christian moral theologians, counsellors, pastors, confessors, and parish priests will almost certainly say that they *are*. So the homosexual *is* in fact being asked to commit a kind of suicide or, at the very least, to destroy part of his nature as a human being. His nature is so made that it demands of him, as in another way it demands of the heterosexual, that he *act* upon his love; and that he act upon it in the manner which is indicated to him by the specific kind of loving that he knows to be his.

The problem which this poses must engage our attention. But before we turn to it, something will be said about organizations, societies or clubs, and agencies which are of special interest to the male or female homosexual. We shall also discuss briefly the present legal situation, especially in respect to homosexual men. Then in Chapters 8 and 9 we shall consider the 'morality of homosexual acts' and the possibility of a viable 'ethic' for men and women, homosexual in desire and drive, which may help them to work out for themselves a pattern of life which on the one hand will not deny that drive and desire, and on the other will require a genuine 'control' of their behaviour in the light of principles argued earlier in this book.

6

CLUBS, ORGANIZATIONS, AGENCIES

Because homosexuals have felt that they were not 'accepted' by the society in which they live, it has been inevitable that some of them should try to organize themselves, in one way or another, to provide opportunities for meeting, to present their 'cause', and to assist one another in whatever fashion might be possible for them. On the continent of Europe and in the United States there have been several organizations which have had such a concern.

This book is not intended to provide a 'guide'. Hence we shall mention these organizations and societies only in a general way, save for one or two which are well-established and entirely accepted in the countries where they are found. In England itself, plans have been in progress for some time to establish clubs which will provide meeting-places for homosexuals; at the time of writing, the exact situation in respect to these is not clear. The project, however, has been to locate such clubs in various centres of population; they are intended to be English parallels to the Dutch societies which will be mentioned later. In the United States, similar plans have been discussed; once again, their status is by no means clear at the time of writing.

However, there *are* organizations primarily concerned to further the cause of the homosexual, male or female. In the United States three groups have been particularly prominent. One is for women and is known as the Daughters of Bilitis. On a recent visit to the United States I had the privilege of meeting a leading member of that society. I found her a highly intelligent and well-educated woman; she was also

F

a practising Christian. She spoke of periodicals, notably *Ladder*, which were published especially for her fellow-lesbians; but she admitted that it was not easy to secure general support for the movement since many women do not care to be identified in any way with a group which would possess mailing-lists, etc.

For men, there are at least two active groups in the United States. One is the Mattachine Society, the other is called 'One'. The former has now split up into regional societies; from what one can gather the New York and Washington and San Francisco branches are particularly active. They publish pamphlets, arrange meetings from time to time, and provide counselling services. 'One', whose headquarters is in Los Angeles, California, has also undergone splits in membership; but it still publishes, in its surviving segments, monthly periodicals, one entitled *Tangents* and the other called by the name of the original group, *One*; it provides opportunities for meetings, has arranged a national conference of homosexuals, and conducts a programme of education with lectures and seminars. Both of these groups co-operate with the women's organization already mentioned.

In the Scandinavian countries, there are well-known societies concerned to promote the cause of the homosexuals. As the legal situation, especially in Denmark, is fairly relaxed, there has been a much more open expression of the homosexual viewpoint. Sweden, too, in recent years, has been a relatively 'free' country for homosexuals. In both of these lands there are several periodicals especially designed for the homosexual reading-public. These include journals such as *Homo* in Sweden, and *Amigo*, *Fos*, and *Vennen* ('The Friend') in Denmark. Furthermore, an international organization created to integrate homosexual groups in Scandinavia and elsewhere in the world produces a periodical called *I.N.I.* These publications have a varied content. They include stories of a homosexual type, poetry, book reviews, criticisms of plays and films, and also a number of illustrations; the latter are often photographs, sometimes drawings. All these journals are for male homosexuals; hence the illustrated material is usually of men or youths, often shown entirely unclothed and frequently with genitalia very visible. The journals are utterly frank, obviously intended to meet the need felt by homosexuals for stories and essays which will be as graphic in their description of homosexual activity as such novels as *Lady Chatterley's Lover* are in their account of heterosexual activity.

There seem to be no periodicals published in Italy or Spain, both countries where homosexuality is generally accepted. But in France *Arcadie* is a very responsible journal, with a variety of articles that often include learned discussions of the etiology of homosexuality and the place of homosexuals in society. Similar papers, monthly or quarterly, appear in Germany and in Switzerland. Their circulation appears to be fairly large. It is obvious that they provide a very welcome outlet for the homosexual population, which can find in them an opportunity to express views and share opinions. The group that publishes *Arcadie* also has occasional meetings for the discussion of the subject, held at a centre in Paris.

It is in Holland that one finds two organizations which are accepted by the whole population as entirely 'respectable' and which make readily available to the homosexual an opportunity for meeting his friends. One of these is called 'C.O.C.'), which is the abbreviation of 'Cultuur-en Outspannings-centrum' or 'Centre for Culture and Recreation'; it has branches in Amsterdam, Rotterdam, Utrecht, Groningen, Arnhem, The Hague, and Eindhoven, with a total membership in excess of four thousand. Although it seems to have a largely male clientele, it is reported that there are some five hundred women members. The other organization is 'D.O.K.', an abbreviation of 'De Odeon Kring' or 'The Odeon Club'. Unlike C.O.C., which is a mutual help organization, D.O.K. is a profit-making society.

C.O.C. offers a considerable variety of services. Among other things, it makes available to homosexuals who feel emotionally disturbed the assistance of trained psychologists, while at the same time it has relations with legal agencies in helping homosexuals who for one reason or another find themselves in trouble with the law. D.O.K. is essentially a 'night club', located in the heart of Amsterdam; C.O.C. also runs such an establishment but that is only a part of its extended programme.

If one attends either of these clubs, admission to which is possible for a foreign visitor on presentation of his passport, one will find a quite respectable and even unexciting atmosphere. There will be an opportunity for members of the same sex to dance together, and there will be some very restrained sexual activity – very mild 'petting', perhaps, but nothing 'obvious'. There will be some prostitutes, although their presence is not encouraged by those who direct the clubs. Bryan Magee, in the book we have mentioned, says that after a visit to these clubs he concluded that 'in every respect except the identity of sex between dancers' and, of course, of the guests at tables and at the bar, all of whom were of the same sex – 'it was a scene . . . witnessed hundreds of times, even down to the details at the side of the dance floor of people sitting at tables drinking out of each other's glasses, or interlocking their arms to drink; or a hand casually resting on the thigh of a partner; the giggling, the flirting, the squeezing, the laughing' – just as in any heterosexual club in the great cities of the world. Mr Magee also remarks than an evening or two in such establishments led him to see 'that homosexuals really do have the emotions and responses towards each other that are normal between the sexes'; and he admits that he began to feel what he calls 'the *normality* of homosexuality' (his italics), which he describes as 'the fact that when all is said and done it is just like what other people do, just a question of individuals who in other respects are unremarkable behaving in ways which are familiar to everyone'. A similar reaction was reported by Monica Furlong in a recent series of newspaper articles written after a visit to Holland and the clubs there.

A quite new phenomenon has recently appeared in Britain and North America. This is the publication (noted in an earlier chapter) in various journals of advertisements by homosexuals, male or female, asking for partners. Such advertising has gone on for a long time in the Scandinavian journals, such as those we have named. The success of this method of finding friends with similar tastes is probably not great; but the existence of such advertising indicates something of the loneliness of many homosexuals, while the wording of the notices – usually expressing the desire for 'real friendship', 'life together with a loving partner', etc. – is one more demonstration of the fact that the homosexual man or woman urgently wishes to establish a relationship which will have about it the quality of permanence. At the same time it shows that love, rather than gratification of sexual pressures, is much more central than many would think to be the case.

Not unconnected with such advertising is the establishment of bureaus for introduction of homosexuals to others with their sexual preference. There are several such bureaus in the United States and in Britain. Either by the computer-technique often employed in 'mating' heterosexual partners or by some other means, male homosexuals are enabled to meet other men, female homosexuals other women. Enquiry has not disclosed the degree to which such bureaus have succeeded in their efforts; but again their existence is indicative of a need like that to which advertising is also a response.

In Britain there are at least two women's organizations whose purpose is to provide an opportunity for lesbians to meet and discuss matters of common interest, to attend the theatre together, and in other ways to have the chance to 'be themselves' (as one leader phrased it) without having to act in a manner not natural to them. One of these groups is 'Minorities Research'; the other is called 'Kenric'. The former publishes a journal entitled *Arena Three*. No such organizations, of a fairly general nature, exists for men.

Probably this is because it is much easier for males to for-gather in 'bars' or 'private clubs' known to be especially for them; they do not feel so strongly the need for an organized group which will both present their case and also provide opportunity for meetings for discussions.

The most important single organization in Britain, con-cerned to assist both the male and female homosexual and other sexual deviates (as they are called), is the Albany Trust, 32 Shaftesbury Avenue, London, W.C.2. This organi-zation was an outgrowth of the society organized to further the reform of the law in respect to homosexuality. It is a recognized charitable organization, with a staff who are available for counselling and who have been doing valiant work on minimal funds. The membership of the Trust's board includes many distinguished names from all walks of life; these trustees and members of the council are not them-selves homosexual but they are convinced that it is highly important to do everything possible to assist persons who *are* so to adjust themselves to society and to live useful and happy lives. Speaking personally, I should say that the Albany Trust is one of the most remarkable institutions I have ever encountered; the selfless devotion, the unfailing readiness to help those in trouble, the willingness to struggle on without adequate financial support, are all highly im-pressive. The 'case-load', which in the days before the reform of the law in respect to homosexuality was rather slight, is increasingly large – every year some five hundred men and women, boys and girls, apply to the Trust for aid of one sort or another. The professional skill of the 'social-workers' is of the highest order; here is no amateur handling of people's lives but an informed and concerned interest in each indi-vidual who appears. The Trust has plans for considerable expansion of its work, to provincial cities for instance; but these plans are seriously delayed for lack of funds to pro-mote them. This is a tragedy and should be remedied im-mediately. The presence on the official board of the Trust of persons of great distinction in literature, politics, art, religion, science, philosophy, etc., is a guarantee of the responsibility of the Trust and its work. I should urge that church groups and others really concerned for their fellow-men and fellow-women come forward to provide the money required not only for the maintenance of the present programme but for its further growth in centres throughout the land.

The Albany Trust is not an organization *of* homosexuals; it is one *for* homosexuals. One of its major interests has been to provide educational opportunities about the homosexual condition. To this end, it has been able to hold conferences from time to time, attended by social workers, medical men, psychiatrists, clergymen, and others. It has also been called upon to provide speakers for various groups that wish to consider the subject. One of the results has been a growing awareness, especially in religious circles, of the need for more knowledge, as well as the provision of occasions when there can be a free interchange of ideas with men and women who are admittedly and actively homosexuals.

In the United States much also has been done along these lines. In San Francisco and New York, for example, councils for religion and the homosexual have come into existence. These have been highly successful in promoting real understanding. The work of the San Francisco council has been supported by the Glide Foundation, a charitable trust; it has been able to do a great deal to further the welfare of the very considerable homosexual population of what in the States is styled 'the Bay area'. Its programme includes open meetings, frequent consultations, the preparation of proposals for legal changes in respect to homosexuals, and even (on one memorable occasion) a dance to which homosexuals were invited. In New York, there have been several conferences, including a very important one some years ago at which clergy considered the whole question, with special attention to the attitude of the church towards homosexual men and women. This was held at the Cathedral of St John the Divine; it provoked a great deal of criticism, but its results were notable in disseminating information and in awakening keen interest in the problem. New York has two or three areas which are largely homosexual; and the leaders of the conference, as well as those who have arranged similar smaller gatherings, are convinced that the Christian church, as well as the Jewish community, has a responsibility for the thousands who live in these areas.

Something of the same sort is now being attempted in Canada, especially in the Toronto area, where once again there is a very considerable homosexual population. I have not been able to learn whether similar work is attempted in other parts of the English-speaking world; but reports have it that in Australia, at least, some concerted effort is now under way, but by a relatively small group, to work for the relaxation of the laws respecting homosexuality and to provide some sort of advisory service for men and women who are emotionally disturbed because of their particular sexual desires in a society which presumably is strongly opposed to any 'deviation' from the generally accepted norms.

In this chapter I have tried to give a very general sketch of organizations of and for the homosexual. But the question is bound to be raised: Is this really *a good thing*? Granted that homosexuals do thus organize themselves in some lands, granted that other persons have organized groups to assist homosexuals, does not this in fact demonstrate that all moral norms are being abandoned and that in many parts of the world it is now felt that 'anything goes', sexually speaking? Much in this book is intended to deal with such questions and it is useless to repeat what is said in other chapters. But I must say at this point that it seems to me clear enough that any sympathetic and understanding person will see that the 'problem of homosexuality', so called, demands attention. The reason for homosexual organizations is simply that people of this type have felt ostracized and condemned. And the reason for the various agencies which concern themselves with homosexuals is simply that failure to accept such persons has often left them helpless in the face of social pressures, not to say social antipathy.

Thus it would appear obvious that anybody of good-will must want to help and that whatever can be done to help is more than worth-while: it is a human responsibility, a human duty, and a human privilege. One may abhor that which homosexuals do, one with another; one may regard them as sadly deviant in their sexual tastes and practices; one may wish that the condition did not exist. The plain fact is that it does exist and that homosexuals do exist. It is apparent that I myself do not share this antipathy, this distaste, and this unhappiness about the homosexual condition and about the sexual activities in which homosexuals engage. But even if I did, the very fact that I am a human being would make me want to be of assistance to so many millions of my fellows. And the fact that I am a Christian would make me even more urgent in my desire to understand them, help them, and do everything in my power to integrate them happily and healthily into the larger society of which all of us are a part.

Mr Antony Grey, the secretary of the Albany Trust, remarked in a wireless discussion in which he and I and some others had a share, that the basic need of every homosexual is to learn that he is accepted as a human being and hence is enabled to become more human. Of course he is entirely right, speaking as he does from a vast experience of counselling. Yet some will say that no homosexual can truly *be* human, for his desires are the very contradiction of genuine humanity. This seems to me so absurd that it hardly needs refutation. But what is more to the point, every homosexual needs – as does every heterosexual – to be released to love, for (as I have argued) to be able to love and to receive love, in mutual affection, is one of the marks of the adult human being. The homosexual's *way* of loving, or rather the direction which his loving will take, is different from the heterosexual's; but that does not deny either his need of nor his capacity for giving and receiving in love.

If this be true, as many of us are sure it is, then the first step which men and women who care for their fellows will wish to take is to try to understand ways of loving, or directions in loving, which are different from their own. That will help them see why there are such clubs, groups, societies, organizations, as have been mentioned in this chapter. They will be able to grasp the patent fact that since society has denied the homosexual the easy opportunity to meet others like him or her, in an atmosphere which is both pleasant and decent, it is inevitable that there will be such groups or occasions for meeting, while in the absence of these the homosexual will seek less desirable and pleasant places to make acquaintances, to *be* himself or herself, and to talk and act easily and naturally. Anything that can be done to help is important here.

For homosexuals are not dirty people who behave indecently. They may be driven to expedients that they themselves in their better moments regret; but generally they do not wish to outrage public opinion. Of course there are a *very* few who do want to do just that; the situation is like that among heterosexuals, where also there are a *very* few who delight in shocking. Mr Grey is right: the ordinary man or woman who is aware of his homosexual drive wants essentially to be human and to be known and accepted as such. *He wants to love*; and when he is driven to the 'one-night stand' or the use of prostitutes he knows, deep down inside him, that this is a very poor second-best for *the real thing*. I have spoken of some of the homosexual couples known to me who live together happily and faithfully; their number is much larger than is ordinarily believed. Most homosexuals want desperately that sort of enduring relationship – or if they are realistic enough to know that under present circumstances this is both difficult and unlikely, they want as enduring a relationship as is possible for them. Only so can they be fulfilled and realize all their potentiality as men and women.

If this were better understood by the public at large, much of what is known as the 'problem' of homosexuality would vanish. For the 'problem' is to a considerable degree the problem of the prejudiced and condemnatory heterosexual. As James Baldwin and others have said about the 'negro problem' – that it is primarily the 'white problem' because it is primarily the problem of white people not recognizing and accepting black people as their brothers – so also with the question of homosexuality. One could wish that Christians, above all, would realize this fact and act upon it.

7

THE LEGAL SITUATION

Everyone knows that after a protracted campaign and with various delays the Sexual Offences Act of 1967 – a private member's bill sponsored by Mr Leo Abse – was finally adopted by Parliament in London and came into effect on 27 July 1967. As we have noted, this bill was supported, in its main provisions so far as homosexuality is concerned, by a very impressive list of public organizations and institutions, as well as by distinguished leaders of opinion. The Church of England, to the surprise of many, was in favour of the proposals, although dignitaries in the House of Lords and elsewhere made it clear that while they agreed that homosexuality should not be considered a matter for criminal action, they still regarded it as a sin. Other church bodies, representing other denominations, took much the same stand. The Church of Scotland was not ready to support the proposals, its General Assembly taking a negative attitude – although recently there has been a considerable liberalizing of opinion north of the Border.

I have heard the new law described as 'a charter for queers'. But that is a very mistaken way of putting it. In order to see exactly what the legal situation now is in England it will be necessary to summarize the provisions of the law, which briefly is an implementation of the findings of the well-known Wolfenden Commission. This Royal Commission, headed by the distinguished educator Sir John Wolfenden, was set up to consider prostitution and homosexuality; its findings and their legal results in respect to prostitution (essentially *female* prostitution) do not concern us, but the Commission's conviction, with very slight minority dissent, was that the legal position in regard to homosexuality was both unworkable and unjust. After hearing an enormous amount of testimony, the majority concluded that a change in the law was desirable and they made proposals along these lines. It was the purpose of Mr Abse's bill, following the failure of an earlier private member's bill because of the dissolution of Parliament, to make those changes.

The present law has the effect of making homosexual acts between consenting males of twenty-one and older no longer a crime. But it insists that such an act must be in private and it makes it clear that if more than two persons are present when it is 'committed', its criminal nature remains, as it also does if there is not completely free consent by each partner or if either partner is under the prescribed age.

There are also other qualifications. The Sexual Offences Act applies only to England and Wales; it does not include Scotland and Northern Ireland. Furthermore, it specifically states that its provisions do not apply to members of the Armed Forces – Navy, Army, or Air Force – and that it does not include merchant seamen on British ships. In addition, homosexual acts committed in public conveniences, even in self-contained and locked cubicles, are illegal, whether or not the partners are twenty-one or over.

Provision has been made that is supposed to 'protect' younger persons. No legal action is to be instituted in the case of an act where either of the partners is under the prescribed age, save with the consent of the Director of Public Prosecutions. It is also provided that no one can be charged with an offence which was committed more than a year previous to the time of apprehension, although an exception is made here in the case of an act against a child under sixteen years of age.

But suppose a man engages in, and is arrested for, some act which the law does not allow. Then the following penalties are directed: for such an act with a person who has not consented, ten years' imprisonment is ordered; although if the person with whom the act is committed is under sixteen and the act itself is 'buggery' (sodomy or anal penetration), the penalty is life imprisonment. If the act is with a person who consents to it but is yet under the age of twenty-one, the penalty is five years. If it is between two parties both of whom are under age, the penalty is two years. For an act between consenting adults, of the permitted age or older, but performed in 'public' – that is, not in private between the two persons – the penalty is also two years. A similar penalty of two years' imprisonment is directed for soliciting. It is also illegal to 'procure' another person for homosexual acts, which may be considered as included in the soliciting provision.

Now this new law has at least made it possible for adult males, under carefully prescribed conditions, to do what they please sexually without offending the law – although oddly enough, in view of the fact that the Sexual Offences Act has to do only with men, it might be possible for a husband to commit sodomy with his wife and suffer the full penalty of the older law. However, it is hardly likely that this sort of thing is regarded as a matter for police action.

There are at least two problems which the new law raises. One of these has to do with its reference to privacy and the obvious conclusion that if there happen to be, say, three men involved in some sexual activity, they are acting criminally. Presumably the intention was to prevent what are some-times called 'sexual orgies', with a number of persons en-gaging simultaneously or successively in physical intercourse of one kind or another. The other problem is much more serious. The age-limit is set at twenty-one. This is a higher age-limit than in many other countries. What makes it par-ticularly unfortunate, as the various arrests and trials which have taken place in the past two or three years show, is that young men are very likely to engage in sexual activity from, say, sixteen up to twenty-one, during the years when they are possessed of a vigorous sex drive and may indulge in sexual experimentation which often enough is relatively harmless, emotionally and physiologically speaking. In any event, when the voting age is likely to be reduced to eighteen, as the legal age of majority (recommended by the Latey Commission), it would appear somewhat ridiculous to maintain twenty-one as the lowest possible age for legal consent for homosexual males.

This last provision – the age-limit of twenty-one – was intended to prevent the seduction of young men under that age. However it is clear enough, from all the evidence we possess, that there are very few male homosexuals who engage, or wish to engage, in seduction of this sort. Despite a popular belief, all experts seem to agree that homosexuals do not as a rule have an interest in very young children and that few of them wish to engage in sexual acts with others who are considerably younger than themselves. But the serious problem comes when two young men, attracted to each other, indulge in sexual experimentation or outright sexual intercourse; if they are under twenty-one, they face two years in gaol, along with all the embarrassment and shame which a trial will involve. Yet a boy of eighteen or nineteen is not so very different from a young man two or three years his elder.

So much for the legal situation in England. We have already noted the lower age-limit in many other countries; we have also observed that in most of these countries, West Germany being a notable exception, the attitude towards homosexuality is much more relaxed than it has been in England. In some of the Latin countries, for example, homosexuality is often taken for granted. This appears to be true in Italy, especially in the large cities, while (despite its rather puritanical morality) Spain seems almost equally relaxed. The Scandinavian countries do not make any fuss about the matter – for good or for ill, the presence of homosexuals is taken for granted. The same is the case in Holland, more particularly since the vigorous efforts undertaken by the C.O.C., to which we referred in the last chapter.

In the United States, there is a great variety of laws in respect to homosexuality; each different state of the fifty which make up that country has its own legal code and it is hard to find any complete agreement. Recently, the state of Illinois has adopted a new law, not unlike that now in effect in England, whereby consenting males of adult age are not criminals if they engage in private sexual acts together. The situation in respect to women is much as in Britain, since for most purposes the laws of the several American states do not appear to contemplate, or if they contemplate do not impose penalties upon, sexual activity between women. In the forty-nine states where all homosexual acts are illegal, the penalties for violation of the law vary as much as the laws themselves – all the way from very short prison sentences or fines for 'indecency' up to long-term imprisonment (even for life, in some places, although this is evidently never imposed nowadays) for 'sodomy' or anal relationships. In Canada the law is now being revised.

Compendiously one can say that the legal attitude in the United States is expressed in the phrase which speaks of 'that infamous crime against nature, committed by man with man'. Certainly this is a highly ambiguous phrase; as Alan Watts remarks in mentioning such a prohibition (*Beyond Theology*, page 80, footnote), 'presumably this should cover a bad haircut, or partnership in a factory that pollutes a river'. But the intended meaning is obvious enough: this sort of language is an older way of referring to oral or anal sexual relationships between men.

But the complete enforcement of any such prohibition is well-nigh impossible. Since nobody can see everything that goes on, nobody can arrest and bring to trial the actions of thousands, if not millions, of persons. Indeed, the estimate has been made that, in the United States, for every single case of homosexual activity which results in some sort of police action, there are at least ten to twenty thousand that inevitably escape detection. Yet the fact that male homosexual relationships of a physical nature *is* illegal in all but one state of the American republic results in producing a sense of dis-ease, sometimes of genuine fear, on the part of men who engage in these relationships. The law does not succeed in its attempt to *prevent* them doing so, by any means; but it tends to develop in male homosexuals in the United States – and in Canada, too, where similar laws have been in force, or at least in effect, as well as in Australia and New Zealand – an emotional attitude which hardly conduces to his adjustment to his condition.

Those who regard homosexual activity as 'an abomination' will rejoice in this fact, perhaps; they will say that since it *is* entirely wrong, those who engage in it should be made to feel like 'outcasts' and 'criminals', certainly like 'sinners' against the accepted moral code. Yet one must ask whether it is right for society to set up a standard which is admittedly unenforced and unenforceable, simply in order to make millions of human beings feel miserable. And what is meant, anyway, when we speak of 'crimes against nature' or 'abnormal' behaviour? Whatever may be the intention of moral theologians in some religious traditions, what such language really amounts to is that certain kinds of behaviour are not practised by the majority of people – the subtle theological meaning of 'normal' or 'natural' as indicating a divinely intended norm or pattern which in *that* sense, perhaps that sense only, is 'natural' or 'normal' for men, is a meaning that the ordinary man or woman hardly envisages.

But it is simply not true that the majority of men and women *never* engage in homosexual activity. The Kinsey Reports, dealing in the first volume with males and in the second with females, have made it clear that in North America, and we may assume elsewhere too, almost every human being at some time during his life, and perhaps for more than a brief period, has had homosexual relations 'to the point of orgasm'. Most men and women do not continue with such activity, to be sure; as the Kinsey Reports indicate, these contacts for the great majority represent but a passing phase or a very incidental experience. None the

G

less, the mere fact that homosexual practices have been so widespread ought to suggest that they can hardly be dismissed without hesitation as entirely abnormal and unnatural in the ordinary meaning of those adjectives. The situation is rather like that in respect to masturbation, where the same reports show that almost every man and a very considerable proportion of women have engaged in auto-erotic acts – how ridiculous, then, to say that masturbation in and of itself is a wicked because an 'unnatural' act. Most people now agree on this point. The old fears have died away, parents no longer go into hysterics when they discover that their son has discovered and enjoyed masturbatory activity, and the wiser clergy do not create panic in young people by telling them that in masturbating they have committed what is in effect 'the unforgiveable sin'.

We have reason to be grateful to the Kinsey Reports, as well as to other well-attested enquiries, for delivering us from the fears and the condemnations which so readily attach themselves in western cultures like ours to sexual behaviour which offends those who forget that, at one time they too were not without experience of the very thing that they denounce. The consequence of all this is apparent. *If* there is to be a negative judgement on homosexual behaviour, it must be able to stand up, to be defended, on valid grounds. It must make a case which can be sustained and it can no longer simply appeal to prejudice, to forgetfulness of one's own past, or to theological ideas that are either too subtle or too remote for the ordinary man or woman to understand them.

It is not certain whether there has been any great increase in the number of homosexuals during recent years. As I have indicated, what *is* obvious is that the presence amongst us of homosexual males in particular has become much more apparent. They are part of the scenery, so to say, as a visit to certain areas of any great city – or even a little observation in smaller towns and in presumably 'non-affected sections' – will make plain. Since such people are *there*, patently *there*, they must be recognized as *being there*. What is to be the attitude taken towards them? That is the question. Homosexuality in our day cannot be hidden away; it is not to be regarded as something we sweep under the carpet and pretend to be non-existent. It is by no means the most important issue of our day, but it *is* a fact. Society must face that fact: above all Christian people must face it, if they make the slightest claim to taking a realistic view of the world.

8

THE MORALITY OF HOMOSEXUAL ACTS

Everything that has been said in the preceding chapters has helped to provide the context in which the question of the morality of homosexual acts can be discussed. Without that context we should have had no hope of arriving at an answer which fits in with the Christian understanding of God, man, sin, and redemption, but is also alert to the vast amount of information we now possess in respect to the homosexual condition. My short answer to the question is really very simple. Homosexual acts between persons who intend a permanent union in love are not sinful nor should the church consider them as such. But that short answer is obviously in need of development; and its implications and applications should be spelled out if we hope to deal faithfully and lovingly with homosexuals.

First of all, it is essential that we remember what the word 'sin' means. If my discussion has been along the right lines, the sinfulness of a sexual act is not primarily a matter of the person with whom it is enjoyed, provided that this person is himself fully and freely consenting to it. There are two things that determine the sinfulness of an act. First there is the *inner spirit* with which it is performed. We have spoken about this at length, pointing out that the inner spirit means the decision to act in a fashion which will promote the satisfaction of the subjective aim of the person in God's love and with the widest commonalty involved in the decision. Second, there is the *intentionality* which is present in the act and which in some fashion or other is overtly manifest. By this last phrase I am not suggesting a public announcement of intention, although in heterosexual relationships this is the ordinary rule and is the explanation of the marriage service's explicit requirement of such a statement 'in the presence of the congregation'. It also explains the publication of banns some time before the marriage takes place. I mean by the word 'intentionality' that both parties to the act understand the nature of what they are doing, its real meaning, the purpose in all true love of faithfulness or loyalty, and acceptance of its implications for both of them.

Since these two criteria are the determinants of the goodness of a sexual act or of its sinfulness, it is important to see how what we have said about the characteristics of human love applies in the case. The two persons must be committed one to the other, in such a fashion that neither is 'using' the other. They must give and receive in tenderness, so that there is no element of coercion, undue pressure, or imposed constraint which denies the freedom of either partner. They must intend loyalty one to the other, accepting what we might style a mutual belonging. They must purpose to entertain in respect to each other an expectation of fresh and new manifestations of personality, which they will not only 'put up with' but which they will welcome and appreciate. Their relationship must involve a genuine union of lives in which each will preserve its own identity and its own freedom, but in which each will also contribute (through the mutuality which is theirs) to the creation and the strengthening of a bond that will keep them together. The consequence will be the fulfilment of each in relation to the other, bringing to more complete realization the subjective aim which is proper to each and to both.

We have admitted frankly that by such a set of tests every human being is a 'sinner', since no human being – save, in Christian faith, Jesus Christ himself – has realized all that it means to be a man; and when I say 'realized' I am speaking not of some mental apprehension but of a genuine *making real* through the whole effort of a life lived under the mastery of supreme love. Yet I have also insisted that what is most important at this point is not the *achievement* of status nor some specious appeal to the facts at the present moment in its imperfection and frustration as well in its failures and deficiencies because of human weakness and wrong decision. The important thing is that the person shall be *on the way, moving towards* the goal, and *open to* the possibilities which conspire to promote such actualization. He is not *yet* fulfilled; he is *being* fulfilled. Man, like the rest of the creation, is 'in process' towards the greatest good; he has not yet arrived there.

Hence the question we must ask does not concern specific acts considered in isolation from their context. It concerns specific acts in relation to the total context, above all in the movement or direction of the human life involved. The *agent* is much more important than his particular and supposedly 'discrete' (or separate and separable) acts. Of course *no* acts are discrete in this sense; no acts are ever separable nor separated; for human life *is* what it is precisely in its bringing of the past to bear on the present, in its contemporary relationships, and in its aim or purpose. Thus I should phrase the *real* question in this way: does this or that act, whatever it is, contribute in its own proper way to the movement of this person to the attainment of the subjective aim which establishes him as the man he is meant to be – always remembering, and I repeat this once again lest what I have just said be criticized as individualistic, that no *person* is 'discrete' either. He is always and inevitably, precisely because he is a man, a participant in the human race and in *its* movement towards its intended goal of a society *of* love and *in* Love. We may borrow a word from biology, and say that every human person and every act of every person is symbiotic in relation to every other human person and to every act of every other person. There is always the give-and-take, the sharing or participation which is characteristic of man's processive nature, just as that sociality is characteristic of the world-process as a whole in and under the divine Love that is God.

How do homosexual acts fit into that total pattern?

In so far as they contribute to the movement of the persons towards mutual fulfilment and fulfilment in mutuality, with all the accompanying characteristics of love, they are *good* acts. In so far as they do not contribute towards mutual fulfilment in love, they are *bad* acts. But that statement is too brief to be exact. For in every act, however 'bad' it may be in the circumstances, there is some element of good. This is the point which St Thomas Aquinas emphasized in his splendid Christian insistence that nothing, literally *nothing*, is *malum in se* – evil in and of itself. One of the grand strains in the Thomist moral theology, whatever else may be rigid and static about it, is its recognition of what I call contextuality; things are good or bad in the *context* in which they do or do not contribute to an end which in itself is judged to be good.

One of my recent correspondents has commented on the obvious sympathy of Jesus with sinful human beings of all sorts and backgrounds; but he remarks that what troubles him is that in addition to what our Lord had to say, and in his actions exhibited, about love as the supreme criterion for the appraisal of human acts, he also said such things as 'Not one jot or tittle of the *Law* shall pass away'. My correspondent cited several other passages which are similar.

Let us suppose that Jesus *did* say things of this type. This cannot mean that in their *explicit* meaning they are binding upon us today. For surely Jesus in fulfilling the law and the prophets was not simply *reiterating* them. Rather, he was bringing out the *true meaning in the divine intention*, which is what 'fulfilment' signifies in this context. In each instance where he is reported to have spoken about that fulfilment of the Old Testament he went straight to the *heart* of the matter. What did God *really* mean when this or that was commanded by him in the past? What God *really* meant was nothing other than that love shall be the 'law' of human life.

Furthermore, even if Jesus himself as a Jew of the first century accepted the dictates of the *Torah*, we can only understand his meaning if we give up altogether the text-proof approach and every other variety of biblical literalism. In Leonard Hodgson's little book on *Sex and Christian Freedom*, published by the SCM Press, there is a searching discussion of the teaching of Jesus as it has to do with matters of human sexuality. This particular reference is a distillation of the wisdom which Dr Hodgson showed in earlier books when he discussed the question of the use of scriptural material for theological purposes, systematic or moral. He made quite clear that it is not so much a matter of what precisely Jesus said in this or that given instance, when its meaning is confined to the specific historic situation in which his human life was lived. The real point is what the state of affairs must actually be, if a man like Jesus, living when he did and in the setting which was his, spoke about God and man and their relationship in the way in which he is reported to have spoken. This, which is an invaluable aid in the interpretation of all biblical material, is particularly apt for our present purpose.

The Jewish Law forbade all homosexual acts. The Jew had a horror of them; and one reason for this is fairly clear to us. The Jewish people were deeply concerned for the continuation of the 'chosen people' in history. Sexual acts like 'onanism' (which does not mean masturbation but *coitus interruptus*) were regarded as 'spilling' and hence losing of 'the seed' which might have gone to produce another Jew who would carry on the people's unique mission in the world. Homosexual acts are not capable of producing offspring; they too were condemned. Furthermore, the Jew was protesting against all moral laxity and irresponsibility. It would be absurd to use his condemnations in a way that would imply that they were a precise disclosure of the will of God. No matter what biblical fundamentalists may say, this is *not* the fashion in which intelligent and devout modern Christians can use the material at hand.

In the New Testament, the Pauline epistles are the place where homosexuality is condemned; Jesus himself did not speak of it, so far as our information goes. St Paul's remarks, especially in the first chapter of Romans, are a reflection of his Jewish background, in which homosexuality was taken to be tied in with the human tendency to idolatry. They are also, we cannot doubt, an expression of the horror which he felt when confronted by the open licentiousness of many of the great cities of the Graeco-Roman world of his time. But St Paul's precise comments on the subject are not infallible. If Dr Hodgson's principle of interpretation is applied, we may very well say that what the Apostle was driving at was the evil of promiscuous sexuality, prostitution, and a general refusal to accept love as the clue to all genuinely human sexual expression.

This discussion beings us to another important consideration. So far as we know and so far as we can judge probabilities from what we see of the divine character and the divine mode of revelation, God never makes verbal pronouncements about moral duty, as many good people seem to think he does. Are the Ten Commandments, for example, a declaration from on high regarding God's demands or commands? Obviously not. We know quite well how those commandments were originally delivered, their historical parallels, the way in which they are the summing up of earlier tribal or Jewish racial *mores*. They represent profound human insight into what God wishes *from* men; they are not oracles delivered *at* man.

Any notion of divine law as somehow revealed to men in spite of their humanity, as if such a law cut across all human insight and experience, is a most tragic misunderstanding of the way God works in his world. And the later idea that there is some moral 'law of nature' which in its *specificity* is known to men is equally an impossibility, however hallowed this idea may be in certain strains of historic Christian thought. As it happens, I am myself very sympathetic to the notion of 'natural law' and can see its profound value. It *can* be the statement in *one* sense that man is 'to avoid evil and do the good', which is exactly how Aquinas defined its ultimate meaning. But what *is* evil and what *is* good? When it is brought down to details and 'natural moral law' is used to rule out mechanical or chemical contraception, to give a very relevant example, it has become nothing short of demonic. For in that case the 'natural law' comes to mean a series of precise commandments which turn morality into a new variety of Jewish legalism of the worst sort.

But if we speak, as Aquinas does, of 'love in our hearts', or of the Holy Spirit at work in men's minds as they think seriously, carefully, and in a prayerful mood about moral questions, then we are on the way to a thoroughly Christian understanding of the matter. This kind of approach gives us freedom in our own day and for our own problems; but it also relates us to the deepest insight of past ages and to the accumulated wisdom of great Christian thinkers. That wisdom and insight is never to be treated as if it were the utterance of God from on high. Yet it will help us in our thinking provided we take it not literally but with utmost seriousness. We must listen to our fathers but we need also to see that even the wisest of them was not infallible. We have our own decisions to make, in the light of the gospel of God as Love in action in the world; and it may be that we shall have to disagree with those ancient worthies in this or that, perhaps in many, of their views.

One of the places where I think we must disagree is exactly in the matter of homosexuality. They did not know what we now know; nor can we blame them for not knowing, since they were men of their own time. Furthermore, the dependence which they felt upon Jewish ideas, as well as other aspects of inherited thought, prevented them from seeing some of the implications of the gospel to which they were committed. They cannot be blamed for that, either. Nor am I claiming that we in this day have come to know all the truth. We like them are the creatures of our times and of our circumstances. Yet *some* things we do know; and it would be false humility to pretend that we do not. One of the things we know is more of what homosexuality is about. Obviously the subject is by no means a matter of complete and precise knowledge; it is in many ways mysterious in respect to its genesis, its developmental aspects, and its physiological-psychological context. On the other hand, we know that the homosexual is like other men. His drives and desires are like theirs, although the sex of the person they can love is different. We know that if the homosexual is to fulfil himself in a sexual way through genital activity it can be only with a member of his own sex. He may try intercourse with a person of the other sex but the result is usually tragedy for both parties. The male homosexual is able to give himself, whole and entire, only to another man, the female homosexual, to another woman.

So much is generally conceded today. But now we come back once again to the question of homosexual *acts*, in distinction from the homosexual state or *condition*.

What are we to say? I have already indicated my own answer to this question. I cannot see that when two men or two women are committed to each other, loyal to each other, hopeful about each other, in such mutuality that each gives and receives, acting with tenderness and with no force or pressure of one on the other, seeking a union which will bring their lives together as fully and completely as possible: I cannot see, if all this is true, why two such persons should be condemned for committing sin when they desire, as almost inevitably they will desire, to *act on* their love – and that means, of course, to engage in physical acts which for them will both express their love and deepen it.

Nothing that I have seen, in the dozens of books that I have read asserting the sinfulness of homosexual acts, has convinced me that they contain much more than special pleading, inherited or personal prejudice, outworn patterns of thought, and inadequate or even erroneous factual data. They say that such sexual contacts are sinful, but most often they seem to be nothing more than rationalizations of a sense of disgust or horror at the very thought of such physical acts. I know perfectly well that at this point some might try to hoist me by my own petard. If such discussions are only rationalizations, what then about my own discussion? I confess frankly that I do *not* feel the distaste or disgust or horror which others feel when they read or think about what these physical acts involve by way of the kinds of contact I described briefly in a preceding chapter. But surely the point is, not whether any of this is *just* rationalization, but how *good* a rationalization it is. I remember Dr Hodgson once saying in a lecture that the question is whether our rationalizations, granted they exist, can stand up to the test of sound reasoning, common sense, knowledge of the relevant facts, and vigorous critical attack. For my part, none of the books to which I refer nor the countless articles I have read seems able to face *that* kind of test.

Whether my own discussion can stand up to it I am not able to say. But at least I can claim that I have tried very hard to think my way through this whole question and that the conclusions which I have reached were not purchased save by 'blood and sweat' and sometimes, I confess, 'tears'. I began with a quite different attitude; I have found myself driven to the attitude which this book has tried to present.

There are one or two other matters about which something should be said. If promiscuity is a denial of that love which is the point of all sexual union, including homosexual union, what about those relationships which are not in fact permanent but yet continue for some considerable time? Here I suggest that the question has to do with the 'inner spirit' and intention to which I have called attention. Nobody can predict with absolute certainty whether any given couple will remain permanently in love; but if the decision in freedom is there, with the *intention* of permanence, it seems to me that the situation is not very much unlike that which is found in heterosexual marriage. If and when all Christian communions become realistic about marriage and approach the question of divorce with something more than sheer obtuseness, they may be able to see that heterosexual marriages can 'die', as our Eastern Orthodox brethren say. When a marriage has died, despite every effort that has been made to keep it going, it is a shocking violation of human personality to pretend that it still exists. George Tyrrell once said, I believe, that 'two cats tied together by the tail do not constitute Christian marriage'. May it not be similar in a homosexual relationship? It has *aimed* at permanence; but the couple find themselves unable to achieve it. One of the jobs of a counsellor or priest ought to be to do everything in his power to keep the relationship going, in the hope that it *will* become permanent in fact as well as in intention. The homosexual pair are at a terrible disadvantage here. Society seems to be against them; they have many problems which the ordinary heterosexual couple never face; they cannot have children to bring them once again to a renewed awareness of the 'togetherness' which will give those children a happy and secure home. But instead of using these obvious facts to destroy the relationship, I believe that those who are able should do all they can to assist in promoting its maintenance. If then, after all possible effort on the part of the two persons and of those who would help them, the attempt fails to be effective, they must separate. For if they do not separate, two lives will very likely be ruined. The same is true also, in my judgement, in respect to heterosexual unions, whatever ecclesiastical authority may say about it.

If the homosexuals about whom we are speaking were made to feel welcome in the worship and life of the Christian church, there would naturally have to be an understanding that they would not engage in proselytizing for this way of loving. The fact is that they are very unlikely to do this in any event, despite a common impression that all homosexuals spend much of their time attempting to introduce others, especially young people, into this way. Yet any parish priest or pastor would wish to be assured that members of his parish and participants in the activities of the congregation would in this respect, as in others, act like ordinary men and women who accept others as they are without seeking to change them. Of course homosexuals might find people like them in the congregation: how could it be otherwise, once the church were ready to accept them and give them a part in its life?

It may be thought that their presence would cause problems for the present congregation. But why? I know of one parish in San Francisco, a city which has a large number of men and women who are homosexually inclined, which has opened its doors to them, always trying to make clear that full membership demands precisely that intention of permanence in relationship of which we have spoken, although not turning away others who wish to attend services from time to time. The pastor is a remarkable man, with great insight and understanding, and has been able to prepare his congregation for what has happened. There have been no problems at all; indeed I have been informed that the older members have been surprised at how 'normal' their new friends were and have been delighted to give them a cordial welcome. In simplest words, that parish is a *Christian* fellowship, thanks to the imagination and charity of its minister. At least one church in London, I am told, has adopted the same policy; there have been no difficulties of any sort. What *has* happened there is that a large number of lonely, sometimes almost desperate men and women in their twenties and thirties have discovered that they are *wanted* and *loved*; in consequence their former easy promiscuity has diminished and a number of them have been helped to establish enduring relationships with persons like them. Is not this a testimony to the validity of Christian sympathy for those of God's children who happen to be different in only one respect from the majority of men and women?

Do I then advocate homosexual marriages, with the usual apparatus of the publishing of banns and some sort of wedding in church? No, I do not; because the homosexual relationship is *not* marriage in the sense in which that estate has by now, as a matter of historical development, become an 'established order'. A homosexual relationship does not constitute a 'family'; the absence of children would be sufficient evidence of this. Furthermore, a homosexual couple could not be 'husband and wife'. We cannot undo our history in this easy fashion. A homosexual partnership is something *different*; that does not necessarily mean that it must be something *worse*. But if we cannot undo our history, we can recognize that new things occur in that history. Unless my own observations are entirely wrong, and the letters that I have lately received (since my article in *New Christian*) from obviously devoted priests and from homosexuals of both sexes are nothing but lies, there is an increasing number of men and women today who earnestly wish to live together with every intention of permanence and in what only a cynic could fail to recognize as genuine love. 'New occasions teach new duties', the hymn says. It would seem to me that we could make it quite clear that homosexual relationships of this sort are *not* Christian marriage in any traditionally accepted sense, and yet *are* relationships which are part of the *given*, which either we admit and try to give a Christian character *or* denounce and reject to 'the damage of souls', as they used to say when I was young.

Is there not the possibility of some kind of blessing which might be given to two men, or two women, who fulfil the conditions indicated in this discussion and who are ready to state their intention in the presence of some agent (the parish priest or pastor, shall we say) of the religious community to which they belong or would like to belong? I know of some clergymen who have been willing to do just this, although I know also that by doing so under present circumstances they imperil their jobs and run the risk of defamation of character and very nasty gossip.

But even if some such privately held 'service', with a blessing, is not now possible, there is surely no reason why such persons as I have had in mind should be refused the sacraments of the church unless they agree to give up all physical relations and promise to be celibates. To ask that kind of abstinence is to put them in the class of 'outsiders'; it is to refuse them the very help they need to make whatever success they *can* make of their intended permanent union. Not a few homosexuals known to me wish very much to receive the sacraments, more particularly the Holy Communion. Some even wish to be allowed to come to that holy sacrament with the person whom they love, to offer their union to God in Christ, and to receive from him renewed strength for living together in the commitment, mutuality, tenderness, faithfulness, expectation, and self-giving that they intend and desire with all their hearts. Are such men to be turned away?

If what we have been saying about the basic meaning of man's sexuality is well-grounded, it will follow that every human being must of necessity 'employ' (if that is the right word for my meaning, which is 'express himself through, use as an instrumental medium, and find enhancement of personality by means of his sexual nature') his sexuality in the fulfilment of his subjective aim or integrating purpose. This will be done in various ways, of course. There will be a few who by what they may call 'vocation' are able to reject all overt physical expression of their sexual nature. The majority of human beings find the mode for sexual life in union with a member of the other sex. For the homosexual the only possible way for sexual activity is with a person of his own sex; for him the alternative is either complete celibacy or a distorting of his own experience and nature by attempting union with a person of the other sex – and in that case, as I have said, the likelihood is that both partners will be unhappy and the 'end of the affair' will be tragedy for each of them.

Furthermore, even those who claim that they do not in any fashion 'employ' their sexual nature are fooling themselves. If such persons do not healthily and openly acknowledge their sexuality and seek to express it in ways such as we have indicated, such as dedication to some cause or task or perhaps another human being to whose service they give themselves, they become warped and twisted in their inner lives. We all know the type known as 'the spinster' – who can be of either sex, let it be remembered – who by refusal to acknowledge sexuality and use it in externalizing activity have become embittered, hostile, perhaps even neurotic personalities. *Suppressed* sexuality is still sexuality; but it is hateful and terrible in its consequences.

Those who urge that homosexuals should *suppress* their sexuality are asking that they should become incipient or actual neurotics. One has known instances where this has been most dreadfully true, in which a man who could love only another man has killed in himself, as he thought, all that drive of his affection. As a matter of fact he has *not* killed his sexual desire, however he may seem to live *a*-sexually; what he has done is to push it deep down inside him, where it festers and twists back on itself. The poor victim of social pressures then becomes sour and warped in his human relationships, seeing *evil* sex in everything around him and losing the capacity to 'live in love and charity with his neighbours'. In such a case, I make bold to say, even promiscuity would have been better; although (as I have made clear) I am not for a moment commending promiscuity, among homosexuals or for anybody else. But I recall a woman whom once I knew, so nasty in her attitudes and so hostile in her responses, that a friend of mine said of her, 'What *she* needs is sex!' He had a point.

The title of a famous story by Tolstoy is 'Where Love is, there God is'. Love can show itself in strange and unexpected places. I am ready to say that in homosexual love of the kind I have been discussing, God is present. He is present in the loving relationship and present also in the acts which express and cement that love. I know quite well that the very idea that this could be the case will appear shocking to many of my friends and to the majority of clergymen. But I am convinced that what I have said is true because I have *seen* it to be true. Such human love where God is hiddenly present always needs the further 'infusion' of the divine Love which we who are Christians believe that Christian fellowship, sacramental worship, and the reception of the sacramental elements can provide. The fellowship and the sacrament are

H

not ours, but the Lord's. Who are we, to 'fence' that table from any needy and hungry child of God? How can we, who are ready to confess ourselves ignorant and prejudiced and misguided men, refuse that gracious gift of Love to any man or woman who honestly comes asking for it?

9

AN ETHIC FOR HOMOSEXUALS

I have said that since the publication of the booklet *Time for Consent?* I have received a very large number of letters from men and women who have homosexual tendencies or know themselves to be quite definitely homosexual. One of the questions which has been asked in many of these letters is: 'What ought to be the moral code of a homosexual?' Or, phrased in another way, 'What practical advice could you give me about my homosexuality and the expression of it?'

This question has been asked, I am confident, in all sincerity. Many homosexuals *are* concerned with what I have styled in the heading of this chapter 'an ethic for homosexuals'. They do not want to drift; they do not want to be easily promiscuous; they want to have some 'code' – if that is the right word – which will be a guide for them. Since so many people of this sort are honourable, conscientious, often religiously-minded persons, since so many indeed are Christian believers who wish, so far as they are able, to live in a Christian way, they want help in ordering their lives.

It would have been possible, of course, for me to take the popular line and say that there *can* be no 'ethic for homosexuals'; they are sinners and the only thing for them to do is to give up their homosexuality altogether or (since that is obviously impossible for most of them) to suppress it entirely, at least so far as any overt activity is concerned. It will be apparent, from all that I have said earlier, that this advice I could not give. On the other hand, it would have been possible for me to say that homosexual men and women should simply go on as they have been going, without any moral scruple whatsoever. To answer in that way, however, would have been to deny the seriousness and reality of the very question they put to me. It would have been to tell them that there is *no* ethical pattern which is appropriate to the man or woman attracted to others of his or her own sex. This sort of response was therefore equally impossible for me to give.

Hence I have tried to make six suggestions, with two points in conclusion. These suggestions, in my considered judgement, are sound and right. Others may not agree, of course; but granted the general position which this book has argued, they do seem to me to follow. I offer them for what they are worth.

First, then, I should say that nobody should simply accept his homosexuality without questioning it. It may very well be the case that one is 'going through a phase', rather than that one *is* a homosexual. Some experts have said that in the world which is now emerging every man and woman will be faced with the requirement that he decide what is his sexual drive. The ambivalence which now attaches to human sexuality, it has been said, is such that it is no longer so easy as once it was to know immediately and as it were without question the direction which that sexuality should take. However this may be – there is much to be said for the theory, certainly, but it is not established – a homosexual in particular ought to come to terms with himself in order to be quite sure about who he is.

Hence a man or woman, especially a young man or young woman, should try to associate with persons of the other sex. He should seek to learn whether he enjoys them, likes to be with them, gets along with them, comes to be fond of them – and all this in such a fashion that his sexual drive has the chance to relate itself to the other sex, if that happens to be its proper direction. But if after genuine effort of this sort, it is found that one *is* homosexually inclined – and for whatever reason, since (as we have noted) the origins of that drive are not at all clear, nor can one simply say that it is a *bad* drive – then the fact should be recognized for what it is.

My *second* suggestion follows immediately. If a person recognizes that he *is* a homosexual – and hereafter I shall use the masculine gender, with the understanding that what is said applies equally to woman – he ought to *accept the fact* as well as recognize it. If one really is a homosexual, one's homosexuality should be taken as a *given*: 'This is what I am. Unless I feel strongly that it is *wrong* for me, unless I am unhappy about it as my basic sexual drive and I want to be made otherwise, I must accept myself as I am and for what I am.'

There is nothing for him to be ashamed about. This the homosexual should realize. He is what he is; although he does not need to flaunt the truth about himself, which would be a self-defeating attitude since it would only cause offence to some and make his own position uncomfortable in many ways. There is no reason to glory in one's homosexuality, any more than a heterosexual needs to glory in his own variety of sexual desires. If there is nothing intrinsically wrong in being homosexual, there is nothing about being one which makes one better than a heterosexual. 'It takes all kinds to make a world', says the old adage; its practical application here is that all kinds should accept themselves and each other. Facts are what they are. There is no sense in wishing them otherwise; nor is there any occasion for boasting.

Third, a homosexual should always remember that *God loves him*, and loves him just as he is. That is the whole point of the Christian gospel – 'just as I am, without one plea', just as I am, as a human being, made in God's image, created by him and sustained and loved by him every moment of my life. Furthermore, a homosexual should remember always that God wants him to be the very best sort of person he is able to be, under his particular circumstances. Antony Grey has told of a San Francisco police official who informed a young homosexual that he was not worried about the youth's sexual drive: 'if you are a homosexual,' he said, 'be the very best homosexual you can possibly be.' That seems to me profoundly wise; it is also deeply Christian.

Not only does God love the homosexual; not only does he want him to be the best person he is capable of being; he is also ready *to help him* to be, and to do, the best that he can be, or do. Unlike some who profess to speak knowingly on God's behalf, our divine Father is unfailingly concerned to assist his children – this is what 'grace' is all about. Nor is God so ready to judge and condemn as some of his representatives. 'There's a wideness in God's mercy,' says the familiar hymn – and that 'wideness' applies to homosexuals as well as to everybody else. Thus a homosexual ought to make the attempt to pray, opening himself to God's gracious influence in his life. He ought to join with others in attendance at public worship, in whatever branch of the Christian fellowship appeals to him. He ought to seek to have some part in the life of that fellowship, without advertising himself *as* a homosexual but simply doing these things as a human being. After all, a homosexual *is* a human being, before everything else; he should act like one, without making a special 'thing' of his own particular sexual drive. Human beings are made to 'love, worship, and serve God', says one of the Roman Catholic catechisms; if a homosexual feels impelled in this direction, he should act upon it, without any fear and without any worry. *God* accepts him; and he may be thankful that increasing numbers of Christians are ready to accept him too.

Fourth, a homosexual should be a *responsible person*. That means that he must not succumb to the temptation to make other people homosexuals if they happen not to be that way. This at once will make it impossible for him to seduce anyone, young or old. He will not be the sort of person who is always ready to make sexual 'advances'; that is bad manners as well as irresponsible conduct. It is as unattractive in a heterosexual as it is in a homosexual. Even in our strongly sex-conscious age, people who are continually making such 'advances' are a nuisance.

Responsibility also means that a homosexual should be careful not to get himself in the position where he will be tempted to act in an offensive way. Precisely because his sexual drive may be strong, precisely because he is often lonely and wishes desperately for companionship, he needs to be more careful than many other people. Perhaps this is part of the burden he must bear, at least in society as it exists today. But it is not an intolerable burden; it is a matter of learning a measure of self-control. There are many aspects of life which one cannot control, to be sure; but this is not one of them. A human being does have some power and capacity to say 'No'; that is the measure of his freedom, limited in extent as it may be. In this respect, Christian faith, with the prayer and worship and sharing in the common life that go with it, can be a source of strength to a homosexual, as it can be to any human being.

My *fifth* suggestion is that a homosexual should try to develop close friendships with persons he esteems and likes. These need not be homosexuals like himself. If they are not the last point has indicated that he should not try to make them such. If they are, there is at least something they have in common in addition to esteem and personal liking. But this does not imply that every homosexual acquaintance has to be regarded as a potential partner in sexual activity. Nor do most homosexuals think it is implied. On the other hand, it is perfectly possible that such a friend, who happens also to be homosexual, may become the one whom the other truly loves.

All close relationships can be dangerous to any man or woman, but that is no reason why they should be avoided. We are meant to live with one another, sharing in life's commonalty; and if doing so involves taking risks, that is only part of the common human lot. Yet it might very well happen that one will find somebody who can be genuinely loved, somebody who genuinely loves in return. And *that* can be an experience for great joy and happiness.

Sixth, if a homosexual does find a person whom he loves

and who loves him in return – a person who is himself homosexual in nature – then a problem may arise. Here is a matter about which, as we have seen, Christian opinion has differed and does differ. Some would say that in such a close relationship absolutely no contacts of a physical sort are permissible. Others would say that they are permissible, provided there is indeed genuine love of the sort which has been discussed earlier in this book. It is apparent that my own position is the second one, for I have argued that to refuse the possibility of such contacts is to ask the homosexual to become what the heterosexual generally would never think of becoming – a celibate for the whole of his life.

But each homosexual must make up his mind about this question. If he thinks that such contacts are desired and practised simply to gratify physical desire, with no real mutuality and no genuine affection, then he ought to make every effort to avoid them – since they may succeed in destroying the very love which he really wants. If he does avoid them, he need not become a cold and remote person. If he is sure that whatever contacts are sought or which happen *are* an expression of genuine love, welcomed by both persons, with the intention of faithfulness, of tenderness, of mutuality, of a union of personalities in giving-and-receiving, he should also be quite clear that even then he should exercise control – not by rejecting all such contacts, but by subjecting them to what might be styled 'the control of love', which delivers them from being merely physical gratification through the use of the body of the person for whom he cares.

There is nothing wrong with having or 'being' a body, nor with having sexual desires. God has made us that way. Nor, on the other hand, is there anything wrong about being vocationally a celibate, who determines to abstain from all physical expression of love. People like that must find some outlet, in concern and care for others, which will prevent a warping of personality and provide a means to express love in actual deeds. For the rest of us, it is natural and right to wish to express and to deepen our loving by some manner of physical contact with the person for whom we deeply care and with whom, in the most profound reaches of our personality, we are at one.

This is what is tragic about promiscuity or 'one-night stands' or the use of prostitutes. Here there cannot be the genuine sharing of which the physical act is the expression and which it enriches and deepens. Such contacts as those, however pleasant and gratifying, can never give a person the love that he wants and needs. Homosexuals really know this, because they know – some of them through bitter experience – that these contacts give a gratification which is short-range, temporary, involving less than the whole of themselves. That is why they are often restless, bitter, 'bitchy' about these contacts; they have not been able to find abiding affection and enduring mutuality from such incidents, even if they have managed to get some physical release and what is styled 'fun'.

My six suggestions lead to a conclusion. The conclusion is this: if a homosexual does decide that with the right person, whom he truly loves, he may engage in physical contacts, let him be sure that these are in fact expressive of his total self, that they are genuinely desired by his friend, and that they promote increasing love between them. I have said that many Christians, even enlightened ones, would say that such contacts must always be avoided; I have also said that a considerable number nowadays (myself among them) would not ask of the homosexual such total abstinence. But the homosexual must make up his own mind about this; and if he has a friend or a 'lover' of the sort we have been discussing, that person must also make up his own mind. Nobody should force himself on another person. That is not love; it is rape.

In respect to those occasional, promiscuous or quasi-promiscuous, contacts into which the lonely homosexual is so often led, often against his better judgement, the one thing to be urged is that there is no reason for utter despair. They have happened; they may have seemed pleasant, physically at least, while they lasted; but they were far from being the best thing, as many homosexuals will freely admit. They are often regretted afterward. The reason for them is usually strength of sexual desire, inability to find or keep a more permanent partner, terrible loneliness, and a deep yearning for companionship, even if it is only a matter of a short period, maybe an hour or less, maybe a whole night. What the homosexual needs to be told and needs to realize for himself is that *God still loves him*. He may think that he has done wrong in seeking such an outlet. Very well. Then he is repentant, as religiously-minded people say. He can make a new start. He can go on, with the intention to avoid what now he knows he did not *really* want. But life is like that, for all men. People make mistakes; they act wrongly; they are tempted and they succumb to temptation. But the heavens do not fall in. Nor should one want them to do so for the homosexual, although unhappily there are some people who rejoice to see such a one in misery or despair.

God forgives men their defections and wrong-doings; that is his 'nature and property', in the words of the Prayer Book collect. God forgives and God still loves; this is the assurance of Christian faith. Nor should it be forgotten by the self-righteous that heterosexuals frequently succumb in the same way, the only difference being that *they* seek a partner of the opposite sex to gratify their sexual desires with an encounter of but a few minutes, or an hour, or a night.

Finally, I should add that the homosexual who decides for a long relationship, as he may hope a life-long one, with another of his own sex, is almost certainly doing the very best thing that is open to him. Nor do I have the slightest doubt that God can and does bless that relationship. The basic question here for the homosexual is whether he will let the human love which to him is so wonderful find its grounding in the divine Love, in God himself. That it *is* so grounded I take to be a matter of fact, so far as Christian faith is concerned – although one knows very well that to some this will seem an outrageous thought. But to *let* it be grounded, to allow it to be consciously realized and felt, requires human surrender. So I should ask the homosexual, 'Will you *let* God bless you? Will you *let* him work in your life and in your friend's life and in the life which you share together?' God made men to become true lovers; he wants them to be the best they can possibly be. To acknowledge this and try to base one's existence and one's relationships on it, in full responsibility, gives that existence and that relationship a meaning and a dignity which otherwise they cannot have.

There is no doubt that many heterosexuals who read this chapter will say that it has been altogether too permissive. There is no doubt, either, that some homosexuals who read it will say that it is too rigorist, not anything like permissive enough. As to the former criticism, my response would be that it is not permissive so much as realistic, and that the whole motivation has been the urgent desire to see the homosexual through the eyes of Christian faith and Christian understanding. As to the latter criticism, my response would be that the homosexual should examine himself a little more carefully. Does he *really* find shabby 'one-night stands', without love or affection, deeply satisfying in the long run? Does he *really* feel content with such quick, sometimes often furtive, gratification? Is it *really* the enriching experience that at his best he desires, yearns for, perhaps desperately seeks? I should like the homosexual to notice that he has not been condemned, judged 'filthy', called a 'pervert', or anything of the sort; he has only been invited to come to an awareness of what it is that *he truly wants*, what (I believe) he is seeking in the loveless contacts in which he may engage.

Certainly no man has a right to judge another. Jesus himself told us this and it is now being confirmed, not surprisingly, by all that we have learned through depth-psychology and other research which shows us that it is not unto *us* (whoever we may be) that 'all hearts are open, all desires known, and from whom no secrets are hid'. But God knows, God cares, God forgives, God restores. Faber may have been a sentimentalist but some words, from his hymn whose first line was quoted earlier in this chapter, are apposite: 'There is no place where earth's failings/Have more kindly judgement given'. He speaks here of *God's* 'kindly judgements'. The notion of 'heaven' as 'up', or even as a 'place' at all, will not appeal to most of us. But that *God*, the Love 'that moves the sun and the other stars', feels 'earth's failings'; and that *his* judgements are 'kindly', in the sense of sheerly charitable because entirely understanding: here certainly no Christian can disagree. If he does, he denies the faith he claims to profess. That is why the heterosexual Christian who thinks that to speak as we have done in this chapter is to be 'permissive', in the pejorative meaning of that word, is entirely mistaken in his criticism. Some of us would prefer to be 'permissive', *even* in the pejorative sense, rather than to be condemnatory in the manner of the harsh and unsympathetic bystander.

I close this revised and enlarged edition of *Time for Consent?* with a reiteration of my plea for Christian openness to the homosexual and my plea to the homosexual, whether male or female, to believe that there is a place for him in the Christian fellowship. What matters more than anything else is that all of us come to recognize that our human loving, however odd it may seem to some and however deviant from socially accepted norms, is always a pale, imperfect, often distorted, never adequate reflection of the only genuine and true loving – the loving which is God himself. Wherever we see love or find love – love that seeks faithfulness, acts tenderly, gives as well as receives, establishes mutuality between and among persons – *there* we see, because we are found of, the cosmic Lover. In Christian faith it is *he*, the cosmic Lover, who dwelt among us, supremely and revealingly, in 'the love of God which is in Christ Jesus our Lord'.